"Cheryl's energy, her ability to motivate, and her nonjudgmental empathy are the perfect combination to give insights and a plan of action. She manages to do this without dictating or demanding a one-size-fits-all approach. I highly recommend Cheryl, her courses, her coaching and, of course, her new book."

Diane K.- San Francisco, Calif.

"I needed to find some answers about myself. My biggest takeaway was the realization of affirmations of truly loving myself, allowing me to focus on myself, my future and how that would benefit those around me."

Joanna H.- San Francisco, Calif.

"Expanding my mind, changing my mind, my thoughts, both physically and emotionally to live the life of my dreams. It really changed the way I think, opening my mind to new ways to think and manifest my goals and desired life. I highly recommend Cheryl works, both in retreats, seminars and in her book."

Pete G.- San Francisco, Calif.

A TRANSFORMATIVE JOURNEY
FROM SKIN TO SOUL

Cheryl Pierce, RN, MSN

Copyright 2020

SOULWORX: A Transformative Journey
From Skin to Soul
By Cheryl Pierce, RN, MSN

FIRST EDITION

Printed in the United States of America
ISBN 978-1-944265-80-9

The views and opinions expressed in this book are the sole expression and opinion of the author, which is based on the personal and practical experience of the author on the matters contained within this book and does not necessarily reflect the opinion, position or views of Foresight Book Publishing Inc., which does not endorse or warranty any claims expressed by the author or contained within this book.

All rights reserved. This book is protected by the copyright laws of the United States of America. This book may not be copied or reprinted for commercial gain or profit.

Permission will be granted upon request. No part of this book may be reproduced without written permission, except for brief quotations in books and critical reviews.

For information, contact
Foresight Book Publishing
Chattanooga, TN 37419

FORESIGHT BOOK PUBLISHING
ForesightPublishingNow.com
Info@ForesightPublishingNow.com

Table of Contents

Preface xi
Acknowledgments xvii
Introduction xxii

1 The Beginnings 1
2 Energy Gateways of the Soul 15
3 Finding Clarity and Focus in Life 29
4 Releasing What Is Holding You Back 57
5 Letting Go 63
6 The Power of the Heart 81
7 Entrepreneurship and Spirituality 89
8 Money and Spirituality 97
9 Productivity 105
10 Spirit of Grace 113
11 Your Soul Must Endure Challenges 119
12 How to Take What You Learned into the World 125

Dedication

*This book is dedicated to my daughter, Dana,
my mother, Cecilia, and grandmother.
They taught me grit, tenacity, faith, hope, and love.*

Preface

Confidence, Starting with Your Own Skin

Take a moment to look at the palm of your hand and observe your own skin. It is made up of millions of microscopic skin cells. Let's take a look inside just one of those cells.

The basic elements of a cell are threefold—there is an outer membrane, an inner mantle (cytoplasm) containing the working machinery of the cell, and a nucleus containing the cellular DNA and its instructions. You have about sixty trillion of these cells in your body, all with different roles and responsibilities. But most importantly, every single cell in your body right now is doing two essential things: It is listening, and it is responding.

Each cell is listening to your environment through its countless molecular antennae embedded in the cellular membrane. This cellular skin interprets the environmental signals and relays the corresponding instructions to the DNA within the nucleus of the cell. Your DNA then responds by activating the necessary machinery within the cell. Compare this process to a ship's captain relaying information from his watchmen or lookouts down to the engine room. If the watchmen spot an obstacle, they alert the captain, and he then orders the workers in the engine room to either open or close the furnaces that drive the turbines, or to shift the gears that engage the propeller. It is much the same inside your body: the molecular switches in your cells tell the DNA which genes to switch on and which genes to switch off. This process goes on constantly in all sixty trillion cells day and night, as long as you are alive. And you are designed to unlock the awesome molecular power stored within your body.

DNA is a natural conductor of electricity. It is extremely sensitive to electromagnetic waves. Even just a slight shift in your mood will create enough of an environmental signal to trigger a response from your DNA. Likewise, a negative or a positive thought will generate a subtle electromagnetic current throughout your body that will stir your DNA into some form of biological response. Hence, the skin can react by manifesting acne breakouts, wrinkles, redness, etc. Most of us are completely unaware of how our moods, thoughts, beliefs, and general attitude literally mold our skin and bodies.

Because of the heightened sensitivity of your DNA, everything in your life, from the food you eat to the people you live with, is co-creating your skin and body via your attitude. Your attitude determines the nature of the electromagnetic signals that reach your DNA. For example, if you are having a bad day and find yourself in a negative frame of mind, this attitude will generate a low-frequency impulse throughout your body. Your DNA will respond to this by shutting down certain hormonal pathways in your brain, and you will feel sad, depressed, or frustrated. On the other hand, if you are having a bad day but can manage to break out of your negative mindset and laugh at yourself, a high-frequency electrical signal will reach your DNA and you will feel lighter and more joyful. Your DNA will respond by activating certain hormonal signals that will lead to your day feeling much brighter.

> *Every single cell in your body right now is doing two essential things: It is listening, and it is responding.*

The problem is a lot of people are stressed, overwhelmed, and uncertain. They are trying to succeed and keep everything together. At such times it might not be that easy to just laugh at yourself and feel lighter and joyful. Are you struggling to stay focused, to get ahead, or to be aligned with who you really are? I will share with you principles you can use to better master your mind and body so you can live energized and confident in your own skin. You will be able to come home to your true nature and create the life and business you've always dreamed of.

Soulworx is a process created to help you heal your mind, body, and soul so you can live a more vibrant, joyful, purposeful, confident, and fulfilling life. Soulworx can take you on a journey from skin to soul so that you can open yourself up to the highest possibilities of your own nature. The Soulworx process is about you giving yourself freedom, and this freedom begins with reconnecting back to your true essence. As this process continues, it will most likely put you in touch with some deep fears. The good news is that you no longer need to fear these fears. Soulworx offers you the opportunity to face and eradicate these fears that stand in the way of your freedom.

Soulworx teaches you to reconnect with the wisdom of your heart and body and trust your own instincts. By re-tuning and rebalancing your energy centers, you can restore the whole energy system to a healthier state of vibrancy and balance. Reclaim your personal power. Reignite your passion, and take your business to the soul level. Release blocked energy that's been holding you back in your life. Rediscover your creative expression and find your authentic voice. Remember your soul connection and find a sense of sacredness in your life.

Our world needs a new kind of human and a new approach to business. Soulworx describes this new human and lays out the possibilities of a new approach toward business.

May success and true prosperity ripple out into your life, bringing you unseen joys.

Acknowledgments

This is the first time I've ever written a book. The first half of this book wasstarted and written two years ago and so much gripping resistance stopped me and so I lost momentum and set it aside in the back burner. Until one day, a family friend saw a picture of me in a New Living Expo magazine alongside some top spiritual authors and teachers like Marianne Williamson, Michael Beckwith, Deborah King, John Grey, etc. What in the world! How did my picture get in there? I'm not an author. I had not made up my mind yet about speaking at the New Living Expo event. Somehow, it feels like the spirit of Grace thrusted me in that direction and decided that I needed to finish writing this book and go speak at the event.

I get it. The message to me is to stop procrastinating and go finish what I started. That I need to share my story to the world, to tell thousands of people that their voice matters and that there is an entrepreneur within them that's waiting to be manifested if only they would trust that little voice in their hearts.

My work would not have been possible without the love and strength of my family, friends, and mentors. It takes a village. Mom, thank you for risking your life to give birth to me and for showing me how to be generous and compassionate.

Dad, thank you for giving me life. Gary, thank you for loving my mom. Theresa Ferrer, my buffer, my trusted confidant, my favorite aunt, thank you for your unconditional love and for always being there for me. Augustin Ferrer, my uncle, thank you for helping raise us up for years, and for your generous spirit. Ramona Ferrer, my late grandma, thank you for teaching me faith, hope, and love. John Pierce, thank you for giving me the greatest gift, our daughter. Dana Pierce, my one and only daughter, the apple of my eyes, thank you for giving me purpose and teaching me patience and perseverance. William and Felix Peronilla, my two brothers who challenged me when we were growing up, thank you for teaching me how to be strong and tough. Maria Angeles Ferrer, cousin, thank you for taking me to my first yoga class and for your infinite wisdom. Eric Douglas Frech, thank you for helping me parent my daughter for many years and showing up in every sport event she joined.

Carla Cline-Thomas, my soul sister, thank you for your bright light and generous spirit, it's always fun reading each other's mind. Maggie Jacobs, my steakhouse partner and good friend, thank you for teaching me that yesterday's transformation is today's ego trip, haha. Jean-Louis Guillou, for pushing me to shatter some old beliefs. Ava Fang, for being the sweetest, and supportive friend. Thank you Steve McNamee, for teaching me to speak up and express my authentic voice.

My Skinworx team, Elsa Calacal, Theresa Ferrer, Sandra Wikholm, Bobbee Calacal, Erin Toni Poole, Kassidy Lanchinebre, Irene Reiant, Paloma Sapien, thank you for being hard-working, supportive of each other, and creating raving fans. Linda delos Reyes, for years of impeccable service before the business evolved to Skinworx. Alexis Ufland and Kurt Houser, thank you for doing an amazing job in helping me create the Skinworx brand come to life. Monte Zwang, for keeping Skinworx budget and projections on track. Patti Biro, for teaching me to understand the retail boutique side of things and making it fun. Bob Beriault, for 25 years of numbers crunching. Jonathan Greye, for your creative social media work.

Thank you Katerina Satori, for inspiring me and helping me prepare for my first online video work, and especially introducing me to Gene Keys. Thank you Maggie Kirkland for your impeccable photography. Lacy Kirkland for helping me with copywriting for my online courses. Travis Shields, my super talented videographer. To my outstanding publishing team, Candido Segarra and Catherine Lear Segarra, for putting the puzzle pieces together. Jamie Adamchuk, for over two years of life and business coaching and helping me breakthrough some limiting beliefs. To my loyal clients, thank you for the opportunity to serve you.

And finally, my life-changing trainers, Brendon Burchard, Tony Robbins, and Master Stephen Co, who trained me to master my mind, to master uncertainty, master my physiology, productivity, presence, purpose, to unleash the power within and Master Stephen Co for training me in Advanced Pranic healing.

Soulworx

Most people know their life is meant for more,
but they don't know
how to find their highest purpose.

At Soulworx,
we help you master your mind and body,
gaining clarity of your life's vision,
so you can live
the abundant life you were meant to live.

Listen to your Soul to
Transform your Life

Introduction

    I believe that we all want to live a happy, successful, and fulfilling life.

    I believe we all have a voice; that each and every one of us has knowledge and wisdom and experience gifted to us that what we've learned in our lifetimes. Our struggles, our trials, and our triumphs can be used to help other people.

    I believe in the power of self-confidence, starting with your own skin. I believe confidence is essential for success in every aspect of our lives. I believe that confidence is not something you're born with but is something that can be developed. I believe that with self-confidence, you can accomplish every goal you set for yourself. I believe the power of confidence will help you overcome fears and tackle challenges. I believe confidence can transform a dreamer into a doer—a person of action—someone who sets their sights on goals and achieves their mission.

    My story began with my being terrorized at the age of four. A caregiver threatened me with a knife, saying she would kill my whole family if I told my parents that she abused me. I hid in a car and I cried . . . and cried . . . and cried . . . as loudly as I could. No one heard me . . . So, I stopped crying. I promised myself I would never hurt like that again, never feel like that again, and never cry like that ever again. For forty-plus years, I bottled up my emotions and kept my promise to myself to not feel, hurt, or cry.

Then a few years ago, in 2012, I started experiencing panic attacks. I felt this smothering sensation as if someone had put a pillow over my face. I couldn't breathe. I felt like I was hyperventilating, as if oxygen was no longer able to reach my brain. These panic attacks went on for months. I didn't want to see my doctor because I knew she would just write me a prescription for anti-anxiety medication, and I don't like taking pills. Medicine would trigger terrifying memories of my childhood. I remember getting tied up in a chair when I was four or five years old and force-fed food and medicine when I was sick or refused to eat.

The abuse I went through as a child robbed me of my sense of self-control and power over my own life. Plus I developed a deep-seated fear toward others; eventually, I stopped speaking up for myself entirely. I never complained, never caused a fuss. I learned that it didn't work anyway. Doing so just made my life more miserable. Instead, I tried to disappear.

I lived my whole life holding in my feelings, my thoughts, my concerns, my dreams, my nightmares. I didn't want to impose my anxieties on anyone. I didn't want to be a burden; thus, I did what was expected of me. I did what I was told. I didn't have a voice. I had lost my true voice. I lost my sparkle, my confidence, and my self-worth during all those years.

Even as an adult, I felt like I was living a caged life. I became silent and pretended everything was fine so no one could tell what was going on in my mind. I felt like I was dying a slow death inside.

Then one day, I had a wakeup call in which I asked myself:

What's the purpose of my life? Why am I here?
Why did I have to go through all of that, at such a young age? What for?

I knew I couldn't change my past but, maybe I could make it right, through closure, for me and my daughter, who was then eleven years old.

So, I went back to grad school and completed my master's of science in nursing. I specialized in skin and wound care, and, in the process, I was amazed how huge gaping wounds could close and heal completely . . . how the body can heal so beautifully. It became sort of a metaphor for my life. I thought, if the body can heal like that, then maybe the mind and spirit can heal from past wounds, too. At the same time, I started reading books on positive psychology. I attended seminars on neuroscience/neuropsychology to learn how the brain works and how it can heal from past traumas.

In looking back over my life, I have sometimes contemplated end-of-life things for when I'm really old, such as, how would I want my family and friends to remember me? How can I give my story, my life, meaning instead of associating it with such emotional pain? How do I make something of myself? Then one day I sort of woke up and promised myself I would get out of this emotional misery. Simple as that. I had lived there long enough. I decided to do what I love and follow my dreams. Life is too short not to. Instead of feeling pain, heartache, and disappointment about my childhood story, I determined that I wanted my family to be proud of me and say, "Wow! Look how far she's come and how she now shows how much we can accomplish if we believe and put our mind to it. Look at the life she has created. She raised a beautiful, brilliant daughter full of confidence and courage. She built two businesses out of nothing, and now she's launching another one."

I never imagined that I would build two successful businesses as a single mom, while also at raising a responsible, confident, and courageous daughter full of goodness.

With greater confidence a whole new world becomes available to you. Did you know that confident people are happier, more successful, make more money, have better relationships, and forge stronger careers? They excel quicker than others, make more money, and are more helpful, trusting, passionate, energetic, memorable, approachable, courageous, productive, creative, joyful, and giving. Why all this? It's because they have tapped into and sourced the power within themselves. They believe in themselves; as a result, they take more risks, are more apt to pursue their dreams, and recover more quickly from failures, hurts, or disappointments. Best of all, they live more fulfilling and meaningful lives.

I believe that you deserve all those things—love, happiness, success, money, and achievement of your biggest, boldest, most beautiful dreams. I believe that you are worthy of them and they, too, are worthy of you.

I believe that what you think is important, and what you say—your voice—matters; how you feel should never be silenced. I believe that the greatest gift you can give to the world is the gift of you, your voice, your story. I believe that it is your job to perform the difficult work necessary to become confident and courageous so you can become the champion of your own life and inspire others to live life to the fullest, too.

My hope is that you will be inspired and motivated to finally listen to your heart and follow your intuition. I hope you will listen to the inner calling of your soul and gain the courage to create and build the business you are meant to build. I hope you can live a purposeful and fulfilled life with full engagement, confidence, and the joy that we all deserve.

"With greater confidence a whole new world becomes available to you."

1
The Beginnings

Sitting at the airport with my two brothers waiting for our flight from the Philippines to the United States, my mind was racing and I had butterflies in my stomach. Although I had many good, happy memories of my hometown of Bacolod City, Philippines, the day I'd been waiting for was being reunited with our mother in California. It had been nine years since she had left us behind to be raised by our grandparents. My thoughts were dreaming of Disneyland and all the fun of the "promised land."

We travelled 7,007 miles. As soon as the plane landed at San Francisco International Airport and we exited the customs area and the terminal, we were greeted by our mom . . . June 24, 1984. It was the most exciting day of my life, like the proverbial happy ending from a book, but it was also a new beginning, a new chapter. Everything was so new, and the first thing I noticed was the fog and the freezing cold weather. "Where's the sun?" I asked. As the saying goes, "The coldest winter is a summer in San Francisco."

Reality set in as soon as we arrived at our new home and unpacked our luggage. We had to do our own laundry and wash the dishes. There are no maids in the house. Back in the Philippines, we were used to having a maid, a chauffeur, a laundry woman, and a house cleaner. Here, we had to learn how to do everything on our own now. Welcome to Reality 101.

When we arrived that summer, my mother took us to Disneyland, Knott's Berry Farm, Universal Studios, and all the fun attractions California has to offer. It was so much fun! However, the fun lasted only two years. I soon started to feel suffocated by my mother's controlling nature; I was on a short lease, per se, such as my wanting to be a foreign exchange student, but she wouldn't allow me to travel. I also struggled with a sense of abandonment associated with my mother's nine years' absence (from the time I was six until fifteen), which I would eventually have to process and reconcile later in life.

My First Love

One memory that resonates from my growing-up years after being reunited with my mother is that we would shop for her skincare and makeup at a major department store. I remember visiting the cosmetics counter, where I immediately fell in love with the world of beauty and cosmetics.

From that moment on, I knew that I would one day be working at a cosmetics counter. I made friends with the women who worked there and, three years later, at age eighteen, I was old enough to apply for work. I applied through Promotional People, a company that sends fragrance representatives to major department stores to sample their fragrance with passersby. Yes, I was one of those women who stop people in their tracks to offer them the experience of layering Fendi (an expensive Italian brand perfume) on their skin. Using a bowl of water I had at the counter, I would begin by gently washing their hands with a body wash. I would then apply Fendi body lotion, followed by Fendi body powder and a spritz of Fendi Eau de Toilette. I was passionate about my work and the product I promoted,

> *This time it was about the evolution of my business, although, technically, the evolution of our business is really our own evolution.*

and it showed in the success I had as a salesperson, with Fendi sales much better than usual when I did the demonstrations. By the way, my Fendi uniform was a black and white design, and I looked like the flying nun.

Upon noticing my diligence and hard work, the cosmetics department manager approached me and offered me a full-time job. Hallelujah! It was a dream come true. My first "real" job was at the Ultima II cosmetics counter, where I sold a product line doesn't exist anymore. It was a classic. I was then transferred to focus on Clarins Skincare, a French skincare line. I worked for them for two years while attending college studying French and Spanish, with my next dream to become a linguist and interpreter.

Two years into studying languages, my college savings funds began to dwindle. So I asked for financial assistance from my mother, who was a single mom raising three children and supporting her parents, brother, and sister. This is typical interdependent Filipino culture—helping the whole family to better themselves. Unfortunately, Mom said she would help me only if I took up nursing instead of languages.

My mother believed being a nurse meant job security, while studying romance languages was more of a luxury, as she put it. However, I was thinking of working as an interpreter at the United Nations and traveling the world, even though I knew that wouldn't fly in her world. In my mother's world, I was not supposed to go anywhere; I was supposed to stay close to family. After all, I was only twenty years old. Out of the goodness of her heart, my mom wanted me to become a nurse and marry a doctor that would mean life security as well as job security. From that moment on, my journey became one not of whom I wanted to be but one of whom I was not. So began a journey in the dark forest walking away from my true essence.

I bid goodbyes to my professors and classmates at College of Notre Dame, Belmont, California, telling them I was no longer a French major but moving to the world of nursing. Dr. Alexander, one of my professors who taught western civilization, , had an aura of the great godfather. He told me that nursing doesn't seem to fit my personality, and he didn't see it as my passion. As he spoke to me, I was choking and holding back tears because my heart hurt so bad. I couldn't even utter a word after that.

For the next five years I attended and completed nursing school. I married a physician (as it was "supposed" to be), and we had one beautiful daughter together. Unfortunately, between his demanding job and his workaholism, he was never home or spent any significant time with us. I felt very lonely with my baby, as well as abandoned and neglected as a wife. We divorced after eleven years. Shortly afterward, I started my own "little" business (a skin clinic), which hit seven figures in revenue after seven years of being in business.

The restlessness, similar to what I had experienced a couple years after rejoining my mom in America, began again when I was forty-three. Something inside me was brewing, and I began to experience panic attacks. In the middle of the day I would have this smothering feeling; it was as if oxygen had been cut off from my brain. I couldn't breathe; it's like I was suffocating. Panic attacks accelerated, and they hit me daily. That's when I started seeking help. I didn't want to see a doctor because I knew they would just prescribe anti-anxiety drugs. Instead, I searched for a psychotherapist. Deep inside, I knew past emotional wounds were haunting me, and they needed to be addressed and healed. I was very motivated to heal this ailment causing these horrible panic attacks. That's why I signed up for weekly therapy sessions the first month, then decreased to every other week, and eventually to monthly sessions.

I "graduated" from therapy after six months of doing the intense inner work. By now I had acquired enough tools and strategies to get by. That is, until three years later, when another bout of panic emerged. This time it was about the evolution of my business, although, technically, the evolution of our business is really our own evolution.

I really wanted to get myself out from under my parents' roof. By this time, I was renting space in their medical office practicing my trade, doing business while under their supervision. My stepdad was a neurologist and my "supervising physician," and my mother was the office manager. We all worked in the same office. Then I found an 1,100-square-foot commercial space down the street, one block from the medical building in which I was practicing.

Realizing it would take a team to create my vision, I hired Alexis Ufland, a spa brand consultant to help me create a business plan. I wanted to learn how things worked in creating a brand and putting it out there in the world. She and I were a perfect fit, and I worked with her for six months designing and developing my vision. My heart felt so happy during this process of creation. My heart began to open up like petals of a rose. I was finally doing what I loved, creating something that I wanted to create. And not under the supervision of "helicopter parents."

At the same time I was in the process of creating this new business, I was in a relationship that had been going on for four years. I would talk about my goals and plans with my beau. He was skeptical about what I was doing. In retrospect I often wondered why I was still with this person because anything I said he would question it. Not that there's anything wrong with questioning my goals, but I felt as if he was afraid for me, just like my mother had been afraid for me. Come to think of it, he and my mother had a lot of similarities in their personalities. Both were born under the astrological sign of Aries, making them bold and audacious. Their voices were louder than mine. Their opinions were stronger than mine. And because of my own fears, I had the tendency to follow and conform, rather than to lead.

While I was in that relationship, I often asked myself why I was attracted to this type of person. He didn't support my dreams (just as my mother had not supported my dreams). We would often argue every time I talked about my plans and

> "We've got to optimize our health to generate more energy."

whenever I was about to leave to attend personal development events. I felt like I had to defend myself a lot, defend my dreams. Finally, I gathered the courage to leave the relationship.

At that point, I realized exactly why I was magnetized toward that type of relationships. He had a commanding, big, deep voice, and he had much confidence and assertiveness—these had been taken away from me when I was four years old, as I mentioned earlier in regard to the nanny I had. Yes, I finally decided to speak up for myself. I finally found my own voice and got back my confidence. And through a night dream, this conviction was confirmed and planted in my heart. Deep inside of me I knew I deserved my dream and my dream deserved me—as if it were my baby. It took a lot of pain for me to finally leave that relationship, a relationship that no longer served a purpose for me.

Lessons Learned and How You Can Avoid the Mistake I Made

I learned to listen to my own voice, my intuition, through the inner voice of my heart, which is the voice of the Spirit of Grace. I was so motivated to heal my deep-seated wounds that I started searching for tools and strategies, leading me to find some guided meditation practices that completely changed my life. My life began to experience small shifts. I found meditation apps to "Heal your inner child" and "Calling of the divine." I practiced these meditations every day for thirty days—first thing in the morning and right before bedtime. That's how motivated I was. I was sick and tired of living depressed and suffering panic attacks. I also realized this seem to be a familial pattern, and I wanted to get out of this destructive pattern.

The most profound experience I had occurred when I attended my first personal development event. This was in 2016, at which time I was in the middle of building Skinworx, a high-end med-spa retail boutique in San Francisco. I hired an entire team to help me make my dream come to fruition: a contractor, spa brand consultant, graphic designer, interior designer, and architect, and I had signed a contract for the buildout construction of my space, for which I needed $500,000. I applied for a loan at a local bank, which sent a business loan officer to my office, where he pre-approved me. So, I believed everything was in order, and, since I had a near-perfect credit score, there wouldn't be a problem moving forward with the building construction.

After I signed a building lease contract, several weeks went by without further word from the bank. Nothing. I called the bank asking why they were taking so long to give me final approval, when the bank's representative told me I had been denied for the loan. What?! How can that be? I was informed that there was a clause in my divorce papers stating I still owned a property with my ex-husband and which was in debt. By then we had been divorced for seven years and, somehow, he had not removed my name from it.

My shock in hearing this news stressed me severely, and hives broke out all over my body. I immediately starting having nightmares of tsunamis drowning me with anxiety. Since no one could help me, I literally screamed for help with my arms reaching up to the sky. "Help! Help! Anybody up there, can you hear me?" I wanted to cry, but I felt so numb I could not even cry—just a huge lump in my throat.

Fortuitously, a few days later I received an invitation to a personal growth and development event called High Performance Academy, that was to be led by Brendon Burchard. I had read all his books and listened to his YouTube channel, and, as the saying goes, When the student is ready, the teacher will appear. Well, he sure did when I needed it most. I told my team that I was going to be away for a few days and that the funds for this building project would be coming soon.

At the event, I learned tools and strategies to master my psychology, physiology, productivity, persuasion, presence, and purpose. It was four days of intense training. On the last day, Brendon led a guided meditation, during which I had a profound experience of seeing a hologram of my fifteen-year-old self talking to me. She told me to follow my dreams and to keep going. I telepathically responded, "How can I follow my dreams? I don't have the funds to build this dream."

She actually responded: "Everything is going to be alright. Promise me to keep going."

She reached out her hand giving me a signal to go! Then I saw my sixty-year-old self and my eighty-year-old self, both telling me in total peace that everything will be OK.

My body began to shake, and tears I had been holding onto for decades began to flow nonstop. I had never had that many tears coming out of me. In fact, after I flew home, I kept shedding tears daily for almost three months straight. It was like a release, an emotional breakthrough, an inner cleansing.

Still, I had this situation in which my loan had not been approved. In fact, my panic grew such that I decided to cash out my 401k. At that point, I was willing to start all over again with saving for retirement. After all, it's just money.

Two days after cashing out my thirty-plus years of 401k savings, I received a phone call from Amex Merchant Financing. The man on the other line said I was qualified to borrow $201,000 and Amex could wire it to me within twenty-four hours. I thought at first it was a prank call.

Amex wired me the exact dollar amount I needed to complete the project and the construction. No one could have known how much I needed for construction, but somehow the universe conspired and mystically made things happen for me. So, with what they wired me added to my cashed-out 401k savings equaled the total amount needed. Skinworx was born!

> "I practiced these meditations every day for thirty days—first thing in the morning and right before bedtime."

One financial challenge remained, however: I needed to pay off the Amex loan in twelve months. I didn't know how it was going to happen but, with strong conviction, I told myself it was going to happen.

All the pain and resentments flowed out of my body as part of an overwhelming emotional breakthrough and a major release. Buckets of tears flowed nonstop; I could not stop weeping. Tears of unbridled joy. I wept and wept like there's no tomorrow.

I was able to pay my team and asked the construction team to build the store in eight weeks because this was it, all the monies I had available. Normally, it takes about six months to build out the kind of business space I had planned for, based on evidence of what I'd seen along the street over the ten years I've been there. Businesses come and go, and this is what I've witnessed. Basically, I was asking for a miracle, an accelerated process. Somehow, I just trusted, with conviction, that this was going to happen no matter what. And it did! The store was built in eight weeks. It was done, and the workers completed it without me hovering over their work. The construction team showed up every day and worked hard to finish the project. Usually, you hear these scary stories of contractors disappearing for periods of time and the work doesn't get done on time—if done at all. Not this team. Blackline Construction delivered. This company has integrity and pride with their work.

Within twelve months I was able to pay off all the Amex loan plus interest. I worked like there was no tomorrow. At the same time, I kept myself really healthy, eating healthy and getting seven to eight hours' sleep. I minimized all distractions in my life so I could focus, although I did juggle work, a relationship, and my well-being. I had great determination and clarity on what I wanted and needed to do, to accomplish this vision.

2
Energy Gateways of the Soul

"The world belongs to the energetic."
— Ralph Waldo Emerson

    Everything is made up of energy. Whether it is visible or invisible, energy is everywhere. In order to be successful, we need to generate more energy. The most successful people in the world are energetic in mind, body, and spirit. The world truly belongs to the energetic and enthusiastic. Louise Hays's quote "All I need is within me now" is one of my favorite quotes because it encompasses everything in the spiritual essence of man. We've got all the energy centers in our body that have been gifted to us by our creator.

Our Dancing Wheels of Energy

    They are called chakras. The word chakra is an ancient Sanskrit word, which literally means wheel, energy wheel. Merriam-Webster defines chakra as *"any of several points of physical or spiritual energy in the human body according to yoga philosophy."* We've got to optimize our health to generate more energy.

Our chakras help regulate a field of energy called the aura. The aura is a dynamic, energetic matrix, which includes the physical, emotional, mental, and spiritual aspects of our being. Just as our blood pulses through our veins and arteries, there is an energy that surges through not only our bodies, but also into our energy field beyond the body.

The chakras are the energetic "gateways" that connect the various layers of the aura. Chakras are the energy centers which spin like wheels and open like petals of a flower. When open, these gateways allow subtle energies to flow freely. Each chakra vibrates to a specific frequency, corresponding to a specific color vibration. A good analogy is a radio with its different wave bands. Like radio waves, the energies flowing through the chakras are invisible to the naked eye.

Every human being has seven major chakras, which are located in a vertical column running from the base of the spine to the top of the head. Each chakra can be likened to specific computer software with programs relating to safety, sexuality, power, love, communication, intuition, and self-realization. When these programs are running properly, they affect our health, emotion, thought, and behaviors in a positive manner. When they are malfunctioning in any way, they can have correspondingly negative effects.

Physiologically, each chakra is connected to physical organs and endocrine glands, the health functions of which are directly affected by the state of the corresponding chakra. The endocrine system is collection of glands that produce hormones, which act as the body's chemical messengers and are necessary for the normal bodily functions attributed to each chakra. These glands release the hormones directly into the bloodstream, where they are then transported to organs and tissues throughout the body.

"The more you empower people, the more you will be empowered."

Our Seven Inner Worlds

The first of the seven inner worlds is the base chakra located at the base of the spine. The base chakra offers the opportunity to explore and release elements of physical health, grounding, and instinct, allowing you to become more connected to the earth beneath your feet. It is the center of survival and safety. Working with the base chakra unlocks blockages around work, money, home, safety, warmth, and food. This is how our most basic instincts for security, which often bind us in fear and grasping, open into expansion.

> *"Don't you ever forget where you came from. Don't you ever forget your story. Your growth is found in your roots."*
> — Christopher Smith

Principle 1: Consider Your Own Physical Well-being to Be Important

The first principle gives you an opportunity to bring health and harmony to your base chakra.

Following are some suggestions on how to embrace the first principle, but feel free to add to the list and make it your own.

- Eat healthy and ensure that you are getting the right vitamins, minerals, and nutrients for your body.
- Find the right amount of daily sleep for your body, and achieve this as often as possible.
- Find ways to relax your body. Have regular massages, acupuncture, long baths, etc.
- Find the best form of exercise that really suits you. Exercise regularly, and also listen to your body to "hear" when it is time to take a break.

- Limit the amount of alcohol or other toxins you put into your body. Also, watch out for the amount of toxins in your food, the chemicals you use to clean your house, and those nasties hidden in your skincare products.
- Learn to really listen to your body's needs. Know the signs when an illness is coming on or when you need to take a break.

The second of the inner worlds is the sacral chakra, which is the energy center for emotional balance, sexual energies, creativity, clarity, and ease in intimate relationships. The sacral chakra controls and energizes the sexual organs.

"E-motions are energy in motion. If they are not expressed, the energy is repressed. As energy, it has to go somewhere. Emotional energy moves us, as does all energy. To deny emotion is to deny the ground and vital energy of life."

— John Bradshaw

Principle 2: Consider Your Own Emotional Well-being to be Important

The second principle gives you an opportunity to bring health and harmony to your sacral chakra. Following are some suggestions as to how to embrace the second principle, but feel free to add to the list and make it your own.

- Find support to help you with any emotional issues you are experiencing in your life. This might be a form of therapy, counseling, or energetic healing.
- Do not keep feelings bottled up. Find safe ways to express and release your emotions, e.g., talking to a supportive friend, dancing, chanting, or journal writing.
- Find a regular practice to help keep you emotionally balanced, e.g., meditation, yoga, Qigong, creative visualization, or relaxation exercises.

- Structure your life so that it is as balanced as possible. This might include balancing your work time with relaxation time, scheduling time alone as well as with friends, etc.
- Create time for the things you enjoy doing, and spend time with positive people who can help uplift you.
- Create an emotionally calming environment in your home (and workplace if possible) by cleaning your space.

The third inner world is the solar plexus chakra; this is the seat of confidence and courage, your personal power of strength and poise. Here you can open to the strengthening of your will and rediscover your own power, purpose, and meaning. The solar plexus controls and energizes the adrenals, liver, and spleen.

"Courage is the commitment to begin without any guarantee of success."
— Johann Wolfgang von Goethe

Principle 3: Endeavor to Take Responsibility for Yourself and Your Actions

This third principle acts as a guide to bringing balance to your solar plexus chakra. Following are suggested ways of activating this principle in your own life. Take some time to sit and contemplate this principle. Then feel free to add to this list and design your own pathway to embodying this principle.

- Consciously take responsibility for your life. Do not blame others, circumstances, or the Universe.
- Keep sight of your own unique direction, ambitions and goals. Take the right actions to achieve these goals.
- Make every effort to be a reliable person.
- Be self-reliant in a balanced way, i.e., not always allowing everyone else to look after you. In the same way, give those around you the opportunity to be self-reliant in a balanced way.

"Maybe you realize that you are already wealthy because you feel grateful for everything you already possess: emotionally, spiritually, with your family and friends, etc."

- Create good boundaries.
- Find enjoyment and enthusiasm in your life.
- Be self-disciplined in your life.
- Recognize that this is your life and really make the most of it.

The fourth is your heart chakra, which is the bridge between the lower and upper chakras. Through the heart chakra, compassion, balance, nonjudgment, and loving relationships can heal the hurt and open you to forgiveness, and we can thus become open to freedom and expansion. The heart chakra controls and energizes the thymus gland.

"Have the courage to follow your heart and intuition. They somehow already know what you truly want to become. Everything else is secondary."
— Steve Jobs

Principle 4: Value the Qualities of Compassion and Kindness

Bringing your life into alignment with the fourth principle will raise your energetic vibration and bring you into rhythm with the heart chakra. Following are some suggestions for doing this. You might also wish to bring this into your meditation and let your own heart speak to you with guidance.

- See beyond people's behaviors and through to the real person.
- Live your life in the most generous and open way that you can.
- Know that compassion does not mean that you must fix things; just being present for another person is in itself healing.
- Do your best to not judge others.
- Be mindful of showing kindness, compassion, and generosity to all the people you encounter in your life. Don't limit it to just your family and friends.

- Remember to find compassion and kindness for yourself. You must love yourself before you can truly love another.

The fifth is the throat chakra, which provides the opportunity to move into self-expression and inner truth. Here you can open to a deepening of honest communication with yourself and others. The throat chakra controls and energizes the thyroid and parathyroid glands. This energy center is a gift of your voice; how you express yourself in this world; your authenticity; and your creativity, such as to create a business if you're an entrepreneur, to create music if you're a musician, to create dance if you're a dance choreographer, and to create whatever else you desire. It's good to speak about your dreams and ambition. Speak them into existence.

"There is no greater agony than bearing an untold story inside you."

— Maya Angelou

Principle 5: Endeavor to Communicate Truthfully

Working with the principle of the throat chakra is an exercise of mindfulness. Because we spend so much of our lives in communication with other people, this principle encourages us to become highly conscious of how we are communicating. We begin to understand that truthful communication, which is clean and wise, and kind and full of integrity, is not only desirable, it is also good for us. When you have a healthy throat chakra, you will be mindful of what you say, and why you are saying it.

- Have the intention of always being open and honest with your communication, and avoid dishonesty.
- Acknowledge that listening is as much a part of communication as talking; practice active listening.
- Speak the truth with love. If you feel your words are going to wound someone, find another way of expressing your thoughts with love.

- Try to keep communication meaningful, not overindulging pointless chitchat.
- Try to not engage in gossip or talking about another person if they are not present.
- Remain confidential.
- Remember the precept of wise speech: "Is it true? Is it kind? Is it necessary? Is it the right time?

The sixth is the third eye chakra, located between the brows and which controls and energizes the pineal gland in our brain. This energy center is a gift of vision—a vision for your life, a vision for your business, a vision for your family, a vision for your health, etc. It is in this energy center where you can envision your dreams, goals, and future. Visionaries have a well-developed third eye chakra. They use their imagination or wisdom through this energy center. The third eye chakra provides an internal movie screen of images, memories and dreams. It has the potential to sharpen your intuitive nature, bring clarity in perception, and expand the mind's eye.

"Close both eyes . . . look from the other eye."
— Rumi

Principle 6: Consider Your Intuition a Source of Wisdom

In working with this chakra, be mindful that energy always flows where attention goes. The more often you bring your awareness to this intuitive part of yourself, the more the energy will flow through your third eye chakra. You can think of the third eye chakra being like a muscle: the more you use it, the stronger it becomes!

- Endeavor to live your daily life simultaneously on two planes—the rational plane and the intuitive plane.
- Commit to regular practices of intuition-building exercises (meditation, guided visualizations, dream-work, chakradance, etc.)

> *Follow and record positive emotions more often.*

- Regularly ask for advice from your intuitive self and then be open to the flow of intuition.
- Learn to trust your own intuition and sixth sense. When it feels appropriate, use intuition even if it is beyond rational explanation.
- Recognize the relevance of chance encounters, coincidences, and synchronicities. See these as signposts to guide you.
- Create a vision for your life. Be clear and focused. Use creative visualizations, dream boards, image boards, or meditation.

Finally, the seventh inner world is the crown chakra. Here, you can open to a deepening of spirit and a more soulful way of living, where enhanced value and depth can be found in the simplest of daily experiences. The deeper the spiritual experience, the deeper the physical experience. The crown chakra brings spiritual awareness to the most basic of tasks, grounding you in the practice of living fully here and now, fully in the body.

"Our soul always communicates to us through the universal languages of symbols, senses, and songs. These symbols, sensations and sounds teach us about our ultimate place in the world."

— Mateo Sol

Principle 7: Value Your Connection to the Spirit of Grace

Aligning yourself with the crown chakra principle is a tangible way of working with the subtle energies of the Spirit of Grace.

- Practice meditation or relaxation daily (even if just for a few minutes). This helps to quiet the mind, making the connection to spirit more accessible.

- Commit to your own personal spiritual practice.
- Consciously attune to the higher plane of spirit, whether by prayer, visualization, or in your own unique way.
- Regularly ask for higher guidance and let these spiritual forces guide you.
- Remain open to inspiration (when you are inspired, you are in spirit).
- Develop your own relationship with spirit, whether this is with God, angels, spirit guides, or simply a higher source. Trust what feels right for you.
- Give regular thanks for the guiding hands of the Spirit of Grace.
- Embody spiritual lessons in everyday life.

3
Finding Clarity & Focus in Life

Whatever thought is held repeatedly and with certainty, will tend to materialize physically. "Whatever the mind of man can conceive and believe, it can achieve."
— Napoleon Hill

"Thoughts are living things. Thought is a vital living and dynamic power . . . The stronger the thoughts, the earlier the fructification."
— Thought Power, Swami Sivananda

Let's now talk about finding clarity in your life. It's about having a clear vision for your life.

How do you find more clarity in your life? First, what's the outcome of clarity? In order to create and fulfill your true personal brand, for example, ask yourself, "Who am I? What am I about? What matters to me? What's most important to me?"

The brand is you. The word brand comes from an old Saxon word Brinnan, meaning sword. Your brand is therefore like your sword—an extension of your spirit that you can wield in the world. Your true brand is your life's work. Your brand is the extension of your personality, your outer representation in life. As we also know from the business world, your brand is your specific stamp or logo that can catch the attention of others. Because of this, your success in the outer world greatly relies upon your expressing yourself and your higher purpose with clarity and simplicity. When you get your brand right, then your life's work can be expressed effectively and fluidly. Your outer expression will be in exact alignment with your radiance and purpose. As a bonus, the result will bring you good fortune and prosperity.

According to high performance studies (from Brendon Burchard's book High Performance Habits), the most successful entrepreneurs in the world actively seek clarity in four major areas of their lives. This is the number-one thing that distinguishes them from underperformers. They're seeking clarity about self.

These successful entrepreneurs are seeking clarity about social interactions, "How do I treat other people? What do I want my relationships to be like, to feel like?"

They're seeking clarity about *skill*, "What's the skill I need to develop so I can deliver more, be better, hone my craft?"

They're seeking clarity about *service*, "How can I be of utmost service to the world in the short time that I am alive? What would I need to do to make this work more fulfilling or satisfying, or to leave a legacy here?"

When you have clarity about *yourself,* what matters to you, you make better decisions that support that, and you're more likely to stay on your path.

When you have clarity about social interactions, about how you treat others, you're more likely to have a great quality of relationships as well as deep satisfactions and joy of life.

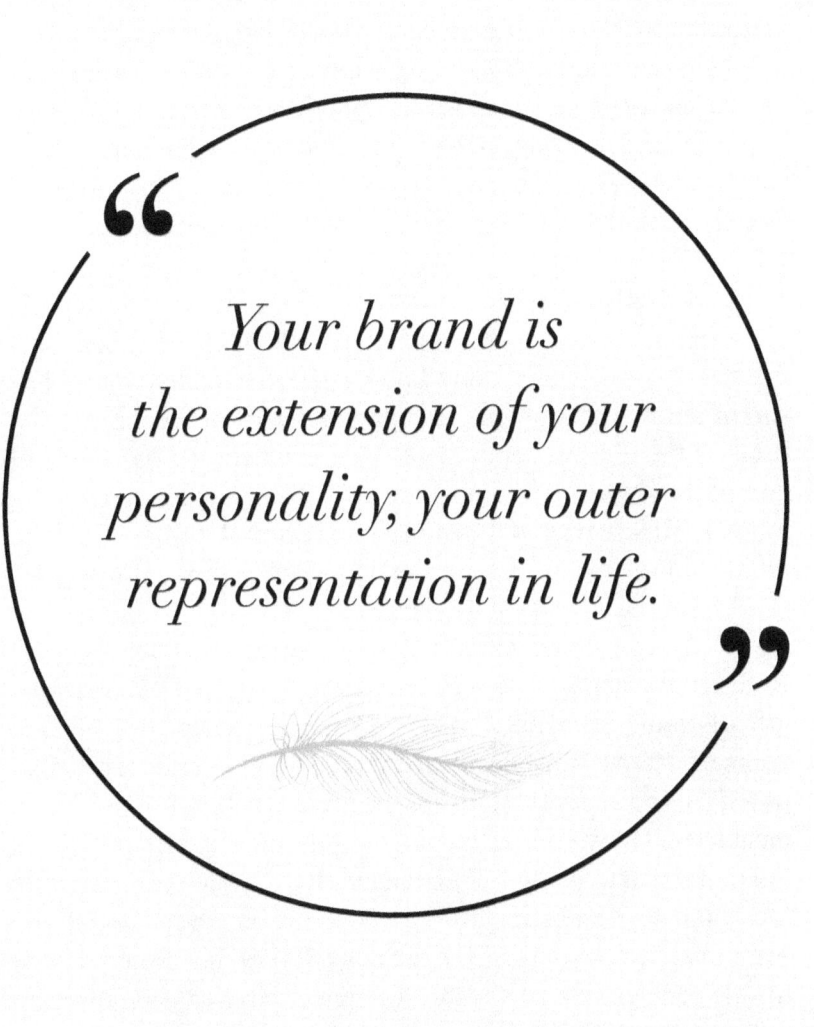

" Your brand is the extension of your personality, your outer representation in life. "

When you have clarity about skills, you're more likely to develop the competencies needed to succeed in your given talent. And when you have clarity on how to serve, you're more likely to feel connected, satisfied, and grateful on your journey.

So how do you develop clarity? Whatever stage in life you're in, whether you're in career transition, or your kids have left the house and you're an empty nester, or you're in school, or you're starting a new business, or you just had some changes in your life, and now you're trying to figure out what's next, here are some simple concepts I learned from one of my mentors, Brendon Burchard, author of *High Performance Habits:*

1. Daily contemplation and rating. This is or measuring your life and for assessing your life. Without clarity, people get frustrated because they don't know what they really want. They sort of know what they like, but they don't know what they want because there're no depth there. This is when you have to start honing how you reflect on your life. This is why you need a journal. This is why you need categories or values that you are rating and reviewing in your life on a weekly or monthly basis.

2. You want more clarity than most other people? Reflect and contemplate more often. Also, give yourself the gift of rating yourself. For example, on a scale of 1-10, ask yourself, "What's my level of vibrancy and energy level right now?" If you're a "1," it means you're dead. If you're a "10," it means you know you're showing up full throttle, bringing joy in the moment and being fully engaged. It's simple yet a powerful tool. Start scoring yourself 1-10, and know which categories you want to measure yourself for each day. Every day. Rate yourself in the categories of health (mental, physical, emotional), relationships (family, partner, love), finances, learning, growth, mission, career, and so on. By observing yourself in these areas that you want to monitor and measure more often, you start to develop clarity.

3. It takes daily contemplation to get real internal spiritual clarity in life. We just don't suddenly wake up one day and have an epiphany in which everything becomes clear. What's going to happen in real life is that you're going to observe your life more consistently more often and reflect more on what's important to you and rate your performance, your passions, and different areas of your life. If you do this consistently over a period of time, you'll eventually realize, "I know myself. I know what's important to me. I know how I'm doing. I know what I'm passionate about, and I know what I love that brings me positive emotion." Not only will you have more clarity but a new level of confidence in life because you know yourself.

4. Follow and record positive emotions more often. If you reflect on the things that happened last week, last month, or last year, you will probably recall that you had many great moments of surprise or joy, and your experienced many good days, new learnings, and victories, yet you did not record them and celebrate them at the time. Those great and beautiful moments happened, but the next day you're back at the grind. You didn't notice there's a theme and threads that give you positive emotion. And what happens to people is they reinvent the wheel every day. Every time they get in the moment, it's essentially a new year; they have no clarity in their lives because it's the first time they're even observing. Follow and record the positive emotions in your life because time is fleeting. Capture those moments and record them. Most of all, feel grateful for them. Then you might even recognize the pattern of these beautiful moments. Have an evening practice of journaling and recording the good things that happened that day, as well as your positive emotions. What did you like today? Write it down. What business opportunities presented themselves today? Write them down. What synchronicities happened today? Write them down. By observing positive emotion and experiences, you're more likely to get clear on what's important to you. This is common sense but not common practice.

5. Get training. This is so vital. People have hopes and dreams, but most of them don't know what to do about them. They've never really had a plan, which is why they end up looking for clarity too late. They're on survival mode. You need a guide to help you get to your destination. Where would you like your life or your business to go? There's nothing that you want to do in your life that someone hasn't already done at an unbelievably high caliber of excellence. Your job is to find that person and get training from them. That means read their biography, read their books, take their online course, or attend their events. You observe those who have already been there before. Start studying them for instruction. It's in training that the insight comes, the "aha" moments and that clarity. People ask me how I got clarity in my career/business. I tell them because I went to so many trainings, and I studied with so many people. I seek clarity and then took massive action.

6. Dive deep into the area of your life. So many people are just skating on the surface of life. They don't have any depth. They don't have any spiritual connection or that level of insight they really want and which feels like the kind of wisdom acquired only through the clarity that can be found only in the depths—the depth in your craft, the depth in your skill set, or the depth in your relationship. When you ask people, "Do you feel that your partner understands what's important to you? Do you feel your partner asks you lots of questions as well as understands, validates, cheers you on, encourages you, and is responsive to you?" People say "No." When I ask them, "Have you tried to cultivate a deep meaningful relationship with them?" What I hear back from them, it's like they're in relationship of proximity, but there's no depth of intimacy or real connection at an emotional or spiritual level. That's because they're not diving deep into the relationship. They're half-hearted about it. They're not all in. When you're really all in on something, you go really deep. The deeper you go, the greater depth you develop. The more that natural intuitive insight emerges. The deeper you go into the moment—that's presence. When you go deep into your experiences and write it down, reflect on it, and contemplate it,

> *It's about experiencing the best quality of life.*

that's when you get the insight and the clarity that goes with being on a spiritual level.

There's an old proverb that says: "Where there is no vision, the people perish." Having clarity and vision is about thinking about your future and what you need to do to stay connected with what matters today. Seeking clarity helps spiritual entrepreneurs to stay engaged in the present, to keep growing and fulfilled over the long haul. Spiritual entrepreneurs have more clarity about who they are, what they want, how to get it, and what they find meaningful and fulfilling. You can learn to develop clarity by seeking and practicing it daily. It is not a special gene that some are blessed to have and others don't. You can generate clarity by asking questions, researching, trying new things, sorting through life's opportunities, and figuring out what's right for you. It comes from continually asking yourself questions and further refining your perspective on life.

My Cost for Not Heeding the Call

My lack of courage, self-esteem, and personal power when I was younger cost me dearly in terms of time, mental health, physical health, and emotional health, the result being that my body developed an auto-immune disorder in which my own antigens, which are supposed to protect me, were instead attacking my system. I felt mentally and emotionally bankrupt. My energy was dropping, and had lost my inner strength.

Dealing with this cost me a lot of money, because I was using certain unproductive activities as a way to band-aid the problem. It was a deeply miserable process of growth for me. It felt like I was disconnected from my soul. Fortunately, though, the soul has a natural instinct to heal itself. Your soul is constantly communicating messages to you through your body, your feelings, your art, your work, even when you are not consciously aware of, or you discard them as nothing more than a casual thought. I had to dig deep within me, perform the introspective inner work, and reclaim my personal power that has always been there available for me to grasp. When you do the introspective inner work, you learn to be assertive without being controlling. You learn how to have authority without ever having to be aggressive.

When you reconnect back to your soul, this vital energy/life force generates inner strength and begins its emergence into your life. You can feel it in your body, as you experience the impact in your life. You should want to get physically fit, mentally fit, emotionally fit, and spiritually fit so that you will want to take in your life and have the strength and energy to follow it through. You will get clarity through *meditation, contemplation,* and *concentration,* which helps you get clarity about the direction you want to take in your life.

Clarity helps you trust your own sense of direction, even if that means not listening to the naysayers. You no longer feel compelled to conform. This doesn't mean that you are being rebellious; it means you are simply being *authentic* to who you really are as you learn to follow your own heart . . . your intuition. Of course, you might still feel doubtful and fearful; but with an awakened spirit you now have an internal gladiator walking through life with you. This inner gladiator's strength lights the way, so you can take risks in confidence and courage. We all need to take risks to move forward toward achievement, to start that business we've always dreamed of, and to make manifest the things we've always wanted to create in life.

Taking the First Step Toward Freedom

> *"I want freedom for the full expression of my personality."*
> — Mahatma Gandhi

We are on a journey here of realizing a potentiality about ourselves. It's through studying and really understanding ourselves that we can understand others, and we can contribute, and we can find the meaning within ourselves. The main thing is freedom—social freedom, emotional freedom, creative freedom, financial freedom, time freedom, and spiritual freedom. We want to be free. In business, in entrepreneurship, we want to be able to create financial freedom. Or, when you go out into the career world, you want to be able to earn a good amount of money so you can have a certain level of freedom: freedom to travel, freedom to have certain kinds of experiences, and so forth.

You also want to have the freedom to do what you want, when you want, and how you want. Inherently, we don't like to be constrained by the opinions of others and what others tell us that we should and should not do. When you dig deep and realize that we are good people and we connect to the goodness of who we really are, you start to really discover the meaning and what is important to you. And it's important to then choose the pursuit or the progressive realization of those worthy ideals and the vision that you have within yourself to create it in reality because it's in that process and actually creating it. So it's both creating it and being in the process of creation of whatever it is that you find that joy, that meaning, that motivation.

That comes from within. Every human has a natural inclination to ascend to higher planes of existence, but it rests upon each of us to match that inclination with real initiative. We must remember that freedom can only be achieved by diligent will and volition. So if you want to create freedom in our lives, we have to make a commitment to ourselves that we are going to do it.

Fear of failure and old, rooted beliefs are two of the major causes of inertia, indecisiveness, and procrastination, which are the enemies of success. If you are made to believe and appropriate the lie that you can't make it on your own because you are not good enough, or that you are a woman, or that you need to marry someone with money for security, success will become very difficult until you change the rooted assumptions you have learned from adults around you as you grew up. I had to overcome generational iniquities.

> *Clarity helps you trust your own sense of direction, even if that means not listening to the naysayers.*

For instance, there were certain patterns in my family, especially the women in my family. I got married because I got pregnant; my mother had gotten married because she got pregnant; likewise, my grandmother got married because she had gotten pregnant during World War II, and so on. As I was seeking inner clarity, that realization hit me, and a "light bulb" turned on brightly inside of me. The first thing that came to mind was, "Something is going on here. There's a *pattern* going on, and I need to stop this. This is terrible. I don't like this. I have a daughter, and I'm not passing this on to her. This has to stop right here with me, right now!" I had great determination to stop it, and at that point the new journey began.

I discovered two books that helped me a lot. The books are the *Power of a Parent's Blessing* by Craig Hill and the *Family Blessing Guidebook: Everything You Need to Know to Have a Blessed Family* by Terry and Melissa Bone. I learned that there are seven critical times when God intends for there to be an impartation of blessing from parents to children (conception, pregnancy, birth, early childhood, teen years, adulthood, and senior years). Most of us missed it with our own children. Most of us missed it with our own parents. The consequence of that is there is a confusion of identity, a wounding that takes place in childhood for most people. In turn, there are consequences that are self-sabotage mechanisms on the inside, causing many of us to sabotage our own finances, our own marriage, our own relationships, and our own businesses.

In my own life, I have struggled with my family relationships, as well as with intimate relationships outside my natural family. I grew up in a family with a parenting style rooted in control, rooted in their belief system, and I carried that throughout my adulthood. My mother had the best intentions of raising us well, and I don't think she ever realized how much her parenting style was affecting us. She was just using the tools she learned from her parents, which were handed down to her as she grew up. The constant instruction of what I should or shouldn't do, or what I should be or shouldn't be, were at times overwhelming, paralyzing, and even confusing. The relentless fight against trying to break the chains of control was constant and emotionally draining to me.

In retrospect, I often wondered why I attracted in my intimate relationships the same type of people I was so familiar with as I grew up. Two of them even had the same birthday! What are the chances of that?

Research from *Psychology Today* magazine revealed that growing up with a strict, controlling parent keeps children from developing the ability to self-regulate themselves. The parent is constantly telling them what to do or not do, impeding their learning, experimentation, and development of cognitive skills. Perhaps that's why a lot of people struggle with their finances because they didn't learn to self-regulate.

Tony Robbins: Wealth Mastery vs. Financial Abundance

Let me briefly pause at this point in my narrative to talk a bit more about prosperity and financial abundance. These two closely related topics are so important to our lives, and yet many of us don't succeed or even attempt to do what's right and necessary to achieve those things—even though they are right there within reach for all of us. This is where I turn to the great motivational speaker Tony Robbins, who often talks to his audiences about prosperity and financial independence.

Here is a summary of what I once learned from Tony Robbins during a recent financial seminar:

"True wealth comes from not only attaining the economic measures you desire, but from experiencing the ongoing feeling of absolute abundance—a sense of emotional strength and happiness, emotions of gratitude for all the privileges we share, and the opportunities to enjoy, have, do, be, and give so many things in life!

"Most people don't master the art of financial abundance because they don't realize that riches do not come from money. True riches can only come from one thing: an affluent psychology.

Eighty percent of success in life comes from your psychology, and only 20 percent of it is from the mechanics of how to achieve. You can learn the mechanics (the tools, strategies, investment vehicles, etc.), but if you don't practice the psychology that creates this wealth, then you will never create lasting wealth and happiness. The truth is you need both psychology and the tools to attain what it is you truly want.

"Creating a psychology of wealth starts with understanding the barriers that can prevent you from taking advantage of all the opportunities available to you. The first barrier most people encounter when mastering their finances is beliefs. Most of us, when we examine this issue, will discover that we have developed a myriad of belief systems that do not support us, or that send us in conflicting directions. We think, 'I don't have the time to master this,' 'This is too complex,' 'I don't deserve to be massively wealthy,' 'I'll deal with it later,' or 'I can't control the markets.' What are the belief systems that you have developed (many unconsciously) that could be preventing you from maximizing your potential? Conversely, what are the beliefs that you hold that are already supporting you or that you can adopt to catapult you to reach your dreams even more quickly?"

"Maybe you realize that you are already wealthy because you feel grateful for everything you already possess: emotionally, spiritually, with your family and friends, etc."

Looking back, I spent a lot on clothes, shoes, and other stuff I didn't need. Years later I came to realize that it was a manifestation of depression and anxiety; shopping was a temporary relief of those symptoms.

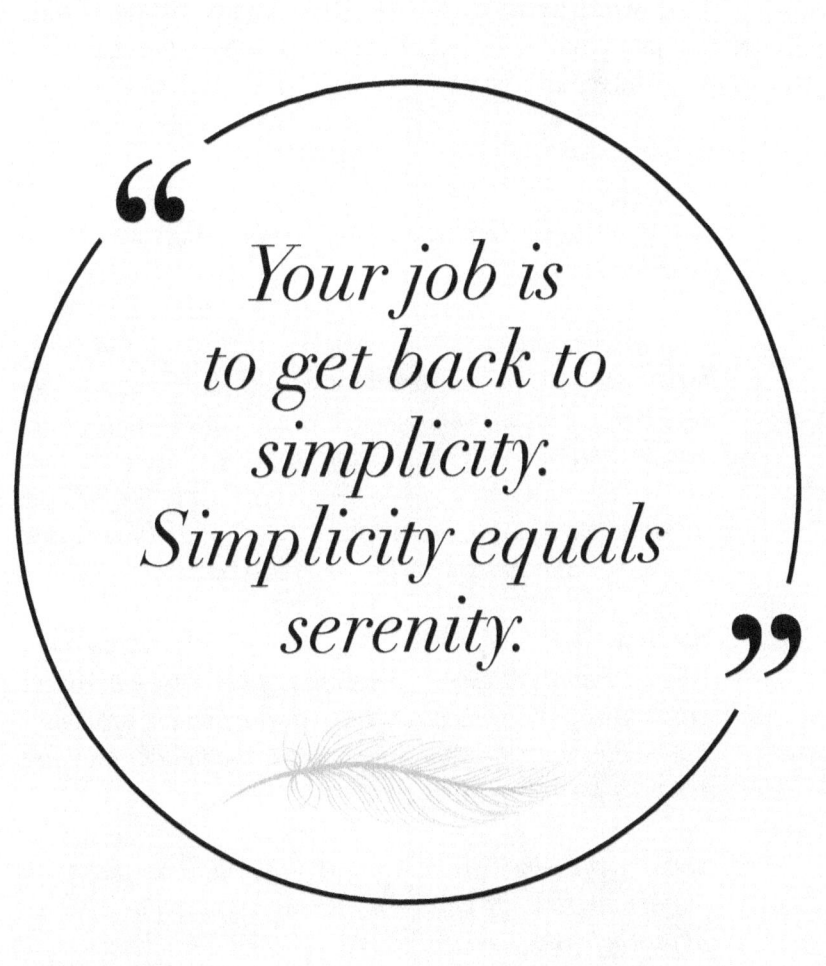

"Your job is to get back to simplicity. Simplicity equals serenity."

Getting in credit card debt and taking on college loans, car loans, and house loans buries people in deeper depression and a caged life. I was unhappy in every aspect of my life—including relationships, marriage, family, issues with power/confidence, career, and spirituality. I was a mess!

One day, I decided to break the bondage of the burden of my past and emailed my family about having a group family blessing. In the email I wrote:

Hi everyone,

It's about time! Time to recover the blessings we missed earlier in life.

The unfortunate truth is that the majority of parents today are not fully aware how vital a blessing can be. We haven't been schooled in this subject and don't understand how to give this gift to our children. Neither do we have living examples to give us a picture of how it's done. As a result, many of us limp through life without the family blessings we were meant to receive.

When we use the term blessing, we are referring to what we call Family Blessing. This kind of blessing empowers you to prosper so you could have a satisfying life journey. These blessings are not rewards for obedience; they are rewards for being born!

Spoken blessing, from parents to children, plays an important role in empowering the next generation to fulfill their life purpose.

So, here are some elements of a blessing:
A spoken message. Attaching a high value. Picturing a special future.

I'll demonstrate it at our luncheon.

The night before the family luncheon, I wrote my own blessing, words I've been waiting to hear my whole life from my mother. I wrote this blessing myself because I realized she had never received a blessing either. First, I demonstrated how to give it by blessing my daughter. I put my right hand lightly on top of her head and said, *"Dana, my only child, you are a blessing in this world, and you are a gift to me. You have a gift. A gift of beauty, intelligence, and a great sense of humor—humor that you're going to need when life gets tough. You are going to have an incredible future. Whatever you choose to do when you grow up, you will be the best in that industry! May God bless you and let his face shine upon you and protect you."* And I gave her a big hug.

Then I asked my mother to read my blessing. I took her hand and put it on my head like I was a little kid. She read the blessing and my body began to shake and tears flowed down my face like waterfalls. I was so ready to receive this blessing. It was a profound emotional release. Then I also asked my aunt to bless me. Then my mother blessed my two brothers. My uncle blessed everyone present. It was a happy day full of blessings, emotional release, and family breakthrough.

The blessings didn't stop there. I bought a ticket to fly fifteen hours to the Philippines to receive a blessing from my father. I also wrote it myself. Words I wanted to hear from my dad, whom I had not seen for many years. I spent a week visiting family, and then on Day 6, I brought up the topic of the importance of family blessings. He was open to it. So, I asked him to read me my blessing. My sister and cousin were with me, so I asked him to bless them, too. We all said a blessing to each other, and everyone burst into tears in a way they had never experienced.

This simple family blessing process is so profound and life-changing! I felt like the powers within me were unleashed—and all the remnants of self-sabotage mechanisms had been dissolved. That was one of the happiest days of my life. From then on, I could see and feel the shift in my life. I experienced an increase in meaningful coincidences or synchronicities, flow, more joy, and abundance like never before. We love coincidences because we didn't make them happen. It's life happening for us and not to us, and it seems effortless. The positive turn of events is accelerated and start increasing. A coincidence that led to something like meeting someone you love, or a business opportunity, or a career or friendship is a beautiful thing. You didn't do it; it happened for you. And when you advance in your spiritual journey by practicing meditation and contemplation daily, you might even be able to speak things to existence using the power of words.

I believe words contain abundant power and can really make a huge difference in our lives. Words can release us from the bondage of abundance blocks, from the shackles of self-limiting beliefs. If you want to finally be free from these blocked energies, you need to learn how to give a blessing and how to receive them. What words do you wish to hear from your parents? Even if they're no longer around, you can still receive a blessing from them. What words do you wish to hear from your children? From other people? What words do you speak to your children? To your parents? To your team? Bless people. Acknowledge their gifts and you will make a difference in their lives. Tell them that they are a gift in this world. That they are a blessing in your life. You will make a difference.

I believe that a family blessing is critical because of all the seven areas that are the pillars of any society (business, government, media, arts and entertainment, education, family, and religion), the area of family is so broken. And when the area of family is broken, all the other areas are broken, too. Family is the basic foundation of all the other cultural areas. That's why it is so important to create a culture of blessing in order to empower people and unify families with the gift of love. The more you empower people, the more you will be empowered. In your business, it's important to acknowledge and appreciate your employees. Acknowledging and appreciating

> *Because of this, your success in the outer world greatly relies upon your expressing yourself and your higher purpose with clarity and simplicity.*

others is like giving a blessing and an action of love. It's all about acknowledgement. The foundation of all influence rests on our ability to acknowledge others, to explicitly share our understanding and appreciation of their experiences.

Learning to Stay Focused

"Where focus goes, energy flows."
— Tony Robbins

At this point, I want you to think about your own life. What distractions do you need to eliminate so you can have more clarity and focus? What are your top three priorities? What is your main focus? The formula is simple: Focus + Discipline + Schedule = Freedom.

So, how do you stay focused? Answering this question is perhaps the most critically important thing you will ever do in your lifetime.

I hope you make an absolute priority to learn and practice how to take back your focus in life, to get more distinct and clearer about what your vision really is. You need to keep it in check. If you keep wandering around distracted, if you keep looking at every new thing that pops up, if you keep trying every single new opportunity, if you keep saying "yes" to everything, if you keep listening to everybody's complaints, if you keep doing everything that they ask you to do, at some point you will lose your life. And I don't mean physical harm or death. I mean that one day you'll wake up and say, "I don't think I've accomplished what's meaningful to *me*. I don't feel like I'm in a job that I care for. I don't feel like I have connection with my family or my friends." At some point, your focus drives everything. It drives your thoughts and your emotions. If you focus on negative things, you'll be negative. If you fail to focus on the things that are important—meaning your priorities—then what happens to your relationships? What happens to the overall quality of your life? Since focus drives everything in your life, you've got to get it back.

It's about experiencing the best quality of life. You need to rein it in—you need to regain control of your focus in a world that's gone mad, crazy, and distracted. So, I ask, how are you going to get your focus back? First, you need to make fewer decisions! Why? As we know from neuroscience and productivity studies, the more decisions we actually make, the more our brain becomes fatigued. This is about you. The more decisions that you make, the more you use the glucose that's fueling your willpower, which in turn is fueling your ability to make more decisions and higher-quality decisions. The more decisions you have to make, the less effective you get in the long-term. It uses too much of your brain's will-power, and it will dissipate and go out the window. So, you want to minimize the number of decisions you're making. How do you do that? Here's some simple tips to consider:

1. Stop browsing on your computer or your phone. Browsing wipes out your focus and your willpower. All those things you're focusing on utilizes your brainpower. and you don't get things done. You start multitasking and doing lots of things, but your work isn't really focused; nothing gets accomplished. So, what happens is your brain gets fatigued. And when your brain gets fatigued, you find yourself sitting with a bag of potato chips in front of the TV and flipping randomly through things online. Do you ever notice that? It's easier to become distracted the more distracted you are. If you're not focusing on one thing at a time, the more problems you're going to have later on to complete one thing. All that browsing, all the tweets, and all the newsfeeds you're reading—every time you look at them, your mind has to make a decision: pay attention or not pay attention? And that decision is costing you focal power and resources later on, even if you don't know it. Browsing social media becomes addictive and fatiguing. Then it's difficult to get your focus power back. Be more intentional when you do things. If you're looking for something, search for that one thing, find it, and stop clicking on all the blue links. Stop swiping all the apps and all the pictures. Do only the things that are going to move you forward.

2. You must define your mission. You need to have a mission for what you're doing today. You need to have an intention for what your next task is going to be. What happens is that people just are not intentional whatsoever, so they end up doing too many things that contribute nothing toward completing their mission. You need to figure out what your desire in life looks like (the goal) and figure out the steps you need to take to get you there (the tasks). By working your detailed plan on a daily, weekly, and monthly basis, your distractions around you will be minimized. Everything else that doesn't contribute to the goal(s) gets a "no!." It's not until you reach that mission, or are significantly on your way to achieving your goal(s), that you free up your time and resources to focus elsewhere. Some people take on too many projects and are not clear in their mission.

I know you're someone who wants to add value and make a difference in the world. So any time someone asks you to do something or you get pulled in too many different directions, you end up being dragged away from your ultimate mission of serving the people you want to serve the most. Instead, you want to remain focused on making your dreams come true so you can support more people, and that means running your business in such a way that you support more people. It's easy to take your eyes off the ball, especially if you don't know what the ball is. Way too often people don't define their personal and professional missions.

If you don't have a mission right now, for this day, if you don't have a written statement about what you're going to accomplish today, a checklist, a goal sheet, a time management tool filled out for today, then you might just as well go to your inbox and let that tell you what you need to do today, reacting to everybody else's desires, demands, and requests, and replying to everyone else's emails.

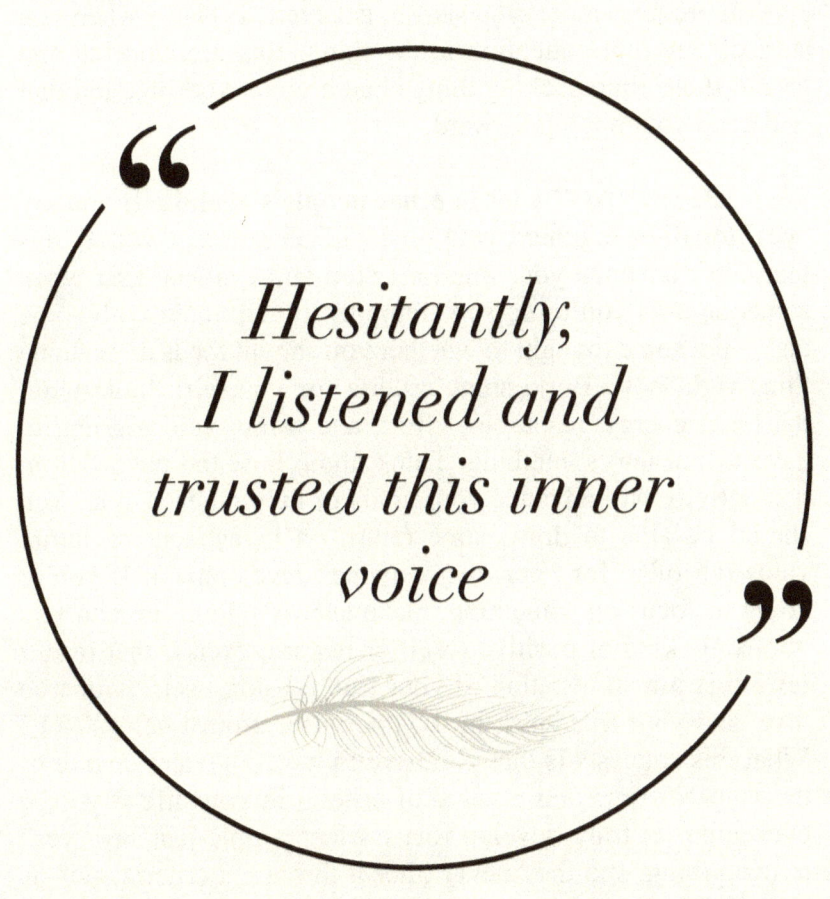

> "Hesitantly, I listened and trusted this inner voice"

Without proactivity toward the mission that you defined yourself, you'll be lost. You'll find that because you never focused on that one thing or moving toward those several things that comprise your priority, focus dissipates or disappears, and you find yourself without progress—stymied and frustrated. Without progress, you won't feel good about yourself. If you want to increase your focus in your life, work toward more progress. As you progress more, you start to get excited. That's when you start paying more attention to the things that are working and less to those time-sucking things that are not working, and that will keep you moving forward.

3. Say "NO" a lot to other people's agenda. If you say "yes" too often to others, your time will get saturated with things that don't advance your mission. Stop and evaluate first when someone asks you to do something or to help them with some task—put some thought to whether you should focus on that one thing right now. Build some criteria for yourself; think about the time, energy, resources, effort, and sanity you're going to have to put into something. Think about how the payoff from that activity will advance your goals or help other people. You should be able to draw some return on investment or future value out of it, for your own personal development. If you're going to focus on something, make sure it's going to lead you into some kind of positive result or reward, even if that result/reward is a manifestation of your true passion itself, your true love, and your true spirit in it. Otherwise, it must get a "NO." What this suggests is that you have to have a greater degree of the value of time and a value of criteria in your life if you're ever going to truly develop focus. Most people just say "yes" to everything, and they never filter it through a criteria such as *"yes/no"* or *"good for me/bad for me"* as a basis for making a decision. Most people say "yes" to too many things: their plate has become full and there's too much to focus on, so they're not even moving forward.

Your job is to get back to simplicity. Simplicity equals serenity. Make sure you're focused on only one or two major things at a time. Don't allow distractions to suck you in. You're moving your life moment by moment, day by day, to accomplish those things that truly engage you, that truly energize you, and that bring you enthusiasm. If you can keep that type of focal power and intention, you will start to experience the Spirit of Grace, which will give you momentum, moving you faster toward what really matters to you and toward your dreams.

Exercise: Focus Discussion:
Answer the following questions:

1. *What areas of your life would you say need more of your focus right now?*
2. *What are your three biggest goals in your personal life over the next three months? Why is each important to you?*
3. *What are your three biggest goals in your professional life/business life over the next three months? Why is each important to you?*

Exercise: Defining Your Clarity:
Answer the following questions:

1. *What do you feel most certain and clear about in your life right now? About which areas do you feel uncertain or directionless?*
2. *What do you value the most in your life right now?*
3. *Do you feel clear about who you are and what's important? Do you feel you're living in alignment with the best of who you are?*

What we focus on and practice more consistently is what we become. Decide who you are by choosing three words that will now define the best of who you are and that will be used to guide your personal life, including your thoughts and actions. Next, choose three words that will now define and guide how you will engage and treat others you meet in life, including loved ones and strangers. Write these words on a piece of paper, tape it to your bathroom mirror, and say them out loud every day. Sincerely absorb and embody those words that you chose. For example, if you chose "confident, bold, and happy," speak them out loud: "I am confident. I am bold. I am happy." Say them over and over again daily, and really practice showing up and acting upon those words that you decided to become.

> *Business is an intellectual and strategic game, but what sustains you and your business is your spiritual strength.*

4
Releasing What Is Holding You Back

Let Go and Trust Your Destiny

Let go and release old belief systems. Trust that there's a divine intelligence within you that is helping you. All you have to do is pay attention and listen to the guiding inner voice. That inner voice is the Divine Spirit within you.

My Lesson on Letting Go

This lesson first came into my life after my profound experience from meditation I referenced earlier. That's when my fifteen-year-old self showed up as a hologram and told me, with conviction, to follow my dreams and go on with my life, which felt like it had been on hold for forty-plus years.

Trusting that the Spirit of Grace will send you the right people at the right time is essential. Trust in the process. Once you're in the right path, you get in the flow. When it's meant to be, things happen faster and smoother and effortless. But when we feel anxious, our breathing becomes shallow, our gaze turns downcast, and our muscles tense up, rendering them unable to receive the abundance that is our birthright.

If You Don't Change Your Focus, Your Energy Gets Stuck in Time

When we focus on the tasks and actions that produce results, a guiding energy will flow. It's very difficult to get to the next level, when we focus on tasks that do not move us forward or don't provide real short- and long-term consequences. You end up spinning the same web over and over.

Have you ever worried about stuff and what you don't want to happen, then it actually happened? That's because worrying is negative goal setting; it's actually focusing your thoughts on things that you don't want to happen. Worrying is like praying for things you don't want. Why would you do that?

I used to wake up in the morning and my mind would start worrying about every little thing, as though it were doomsday. And I would often wonder why the day had not even started, and yet there I was waking up in panic mode. My heart would pound to the point where it was hard to breathe; it felt like the whole world was going to crumble and fall apart. And everything that I was unhappy about would come to the surface, causing weird sensations at the back of my head. All these thought forms made me panicky. In order to overcome this, I began searching on YouTube and found all these amazing transformational speakers; the first one I grabbed onto was Les Brown and his "Power of Purpose." What a powerful speaker, and he was hilarious, too. So, I would listen to him every day just to change my focus.

Then I discovered Brendon Burchard's YouTube channel, and I began listening to him every day while having breakfast. His message resonated with me, so I bought his books and an online course. He made such a difference in my life and energy, so I attended an event of his that was near my hometown.

> When we focus
> on the tasks and actions
> that produce results, a
> guiding energy will flow.

I started focusing on my personal growth and development and how I could get to the next level of mindset as well as master areas of my life such as clarity, energy, courage, productivity, and influence. Once we master these, we can live a more purposeful and fulfilled life.

When you focus on something, you are putting energy on that thing. Along those lines, think about what you would like to come into your life. Focus on that, write it down, and set that intention with determination. Trust that it will come to you in a way that will amaze you. Believe that you are guided and supported and that you deserve your dreams.

Changing Negative Outlooks in Your Life

Are you feeling anxious and/or depressed? Low energy levels? Negative outlooks attract negative people and situations, thus, to change the negative outlooks in your belief system:

Know Where They Came From

If you feel like you're not good enough or you don't deserve or you have a limiting belief about yourself, ask where those beliefs came from? What triggered the thought or belief? Remember that the first seven years of your lives is when your programming occurred: Where did your worldviews come from (politics, self-esteem, values, religious views, risk, wealth and poverty, etc.)?

Until age seven, our brains are in theta brain wave, which is a hypnotic state in which everything is constantly recorded as the five senses receive, interpret, and capture information from the external environment. So, everything your caregiver (mother, father, etc.) said, felt, and did has been programmed into your subconscious mind. That's why we now have certain behaviors, traits and worldviews that might be part of our belief system. Whether we like it or not, we have inherited them. Just like when you buy computers or cell phones—they already come with embedded apps and programs, and so did we.

Changing your Programming

Fortunately, you can delete and replace those old programs. Just like with your computers and cell phones, you can delete those apps and leave only those things that bring you a state of harmony with the external environment and emotions and success in your life (any way you define it).

Changing our programming is a process that can be quite effective. I've practiced this in my own life since 2016, and it has created major shifts in my life and business.

Following are some exercises/practices to generate more positive energy shifts for you:

- Gratitude prayer: count your blessings in every area of your life
- Meditate as part of your morning routine.
- Send the energy of love, compassion, and forgiveness to people who have hurt you.
- Ask your heart for guidance. Your heart is the hotline to your soul.

You need to win the morning by having a consistent routine. Exercise, hydration, gratitude, love, compassion, and forgiveness meditation are life-changing practices, because these daily routines produce frequency shifts in your energy field. Life is like a boomerang, the more positive energy and thought you send out, the more love and positive things you will receive from life.

5
Letting Go

A few weeks after I had outgrown and left a four-year relationship, I heard an inner voice asking me to sell my place and move in with my mother and begin healing work; this would be to heal our relationship, and to forgive and move on. Hesitantly, I listened and trusted this inner voice, and I took action right away. I sold my condominium, half my clothes, shoes, and jewelries.

That was the toughest decision I had ever made up until that time. For a long time, I had avoided spending time with my mother because I had all these resentments toward her that had been simmering for decades. I blamed her for my misery—such as how, when I was four years old, she did not believe me when I told her I was being physically abused by our nanny when she was not around. Eek! And the programming, the belief systems that she passed on to me, was so disempowering! I know that her belief system had been passed on to her, too. That's when I realized and decided these generational iniquities, this ancestral wound, must stop right there with me. I didn't want this to pass it on to my daughter and her to the next generation.

After living with my mother for six months, I thought to myself, "I really need to get out of here." Six months is enough time to make amends, and we actually bonded during the last few weeks I lived with her. During my stay, I realized she was not going to change at seventy years of age. I was the one who needed to change. I was the one who would have to stretch my patience even more. I was the one who would demonstrate compassion and forgiveness. It all started with me.

I asked God where I was going to live next, sharing with him that I would love to be by water, wildlife, or the mountains in the next place I lived, a place where it would be peaceful. Then I Google-searched apartments for rent, and the first thing that popped up was the Lagoons in the Peninsula. Immediately, I called the number and scheduled an appointment to see the available apartment.

On my way there, I asked God to show me a sign if it was the right place for me. As soon as I walked into the lobby of the leasing office, I saw a huge sign on the wall that said, "I am home." I felt my heart jump with joy as my jaw dropped in awe. When the manager showed me the available apartment, I walked out onto the balcony facing the beautiful blue lagoon with ducks, Canadian geese, heron, the great white Ibis—all kinds of birds, with a backdrop lined with a mountain. How amazing God is! Everything I requested came true. It's like I spoke it into existence. I feel like this was my reward for trusting this inner voice.

Once I moved in, I heard this little voice again, saying to let go of my sofa and TV. I had held onto them for a few months before finally realizing I don't use them anyways and they're taking up so much space. This big, bulky piece of furniture was taking up half the living room, and it had been at least two years since I had turned on the black box sitting across the room, taking up space. So I sold both of those things and turned my living room into a sacred space—a meditation room with an altar.

> *Money is only a burden if you give it weight. It's the same with anything else. Money can either trap you or it can set you free.*

Let go and surrender.

1. Letting go: As I settled into my new apartment, I went through my closet and assessed all the clothes, shoes, and costume jewelry I owned. I definitely had an abundance of all those things. Have you ever read the best-selling book by *Marie Kondo, The Life-Changing Magic of Tidying Up?* The KonMari method is a system of simplifying and organizing your home by getting rid of physical items that do not bring joy into your life. Her system really works! It's doable, efficient, effective, and maintainable. I decided to sell my excess clothes online in one of those consignment online stores, and, to my surprise, most of them sold. Amazing! When it is meant to be just flows effortlessly. So, next time you tidy up your place, ask yourself if that item sparks joy. If not, say thank you and let it go!

After all, the freedom of letting go comes when we realize that some people and circumstances might be part of our history, but they don't need to be part of our destiny. Destiny is based on the choices we make, moment by moment.

2. Follow the Signs: When you are lost, all you need to do is ask for a sign or for direction. Sometimes we forget to ask, and we tend to control things and do things all on our own without realizing there's so much help in the inner world, the spiritual world, whatever world you call it.

Divine signs can appear before, during, or after significant events in your life or simply when you ask for them. Signs bring hope and comfort when you feel alone and disconnected, or when you need encouragement. For this reason, know that when you see a divine sign, you are being helped and assisted by the Spirit of Grace. The Spirit of Grace is always by your side and is there to help you fulfill your life mission. It guides you safely on your path by sending you clues. Specifically, it does this by communicating through signs and symbols such as repeating numbers, feathers, coins, rainbows, clouds, tingling sensations, smells, orbs of light, epiphanies, animals, dreams, and even song lyrics. All you have to do is pay attention to these signs and understand the meaning of their (angelic) messages. You are always assisted throughout your journey. You just need to ask for help and have faith that what you need will come in unexpected ways. You have complete Divine support.

When you're in disbelief about your life path, or when you question whether you've made the right decision, seeing divine signs is a clear indication that you need to trust how your life unfolds. These signs serve as reminders of encouragement for you to persevere and push yourself to become the best version you can be.

What Should You Do Next When You See a Sign from the Divine?

Have an attitude of gratitude for the divine's love and assistance when you receive a sign. If you feel uncertain, ask the Spirit of Grace for clear signs and messages so it will be easy for you to understand. You can ask in silence or out loud and be patient, as the answer you seek will be revealed to you at the right time. To help you develop your relationship with the Spirit of Grace and to become more in tune with her presence, below are some basic ways for you to receive her signs and messages:

- **Pray and meditate:** Remember this: when you pray, you are talking to God, and when you meditate you are listening to his answers. In meditation, you realize that when you focus on your breath as you inhale divine energy, you inhale peace into your body; you trigger an action that allows peace to push out all your worries from your body. In this process, you are enveloped in peace in order to hear the answers you seek. Listen with your heart.

- **Journal or write letters:** Express your feelings and desires into words to the Spirit of Grace. You can keep your written words in a safe place or "mail" them to the universe by burning them. By expressing your feelings, you are communicating your desires to your spiritual divine team. Imagine and have faith that you will receive the answers you seek. Express your soul!

• **Light candles:** Light candles to physically remind you that the Divine Light is already within you. You don't have to seek the light because you are the light. God is within you, and you are within God. Because you are one with God, lighting a candle is a reminder of your oneness. Just like the Creator, shine your light wherever you go and be the guide for peace.

It's just a matter of being presently quiet and tuning in to the signs and messages by paying attention to everything that happens around you. There are clues everywhere on your journey. Whenever you see signs, rest assured that they are divine messages of love and light to help guide you on your path safely.

I remember asking the Spirit of Grace to show me a sign that I'm on the right path, that the apartment complex I found on the internet was the right place for me to live in and that I didn't have the time to search and search for a place. Seeing that "I Am Home" sign on the wall was the sign I had asked for.

When I was having self-doubt about signing the lease for the building where I was going to open my business, I saw a message printed on a T-shirt that said, "Don't worry. We got this." And as I walked to my appointment, I saw a sign on the curbside: "Just believe." Signs are everywhere; you just need to pay attention and be aware of the messages. *All you have to do is ask.*

3. Surrender: The next step is to surrender. When you see the obvious signs that are meant for you, the key is to surrender and then take massive action. This is the key to getting to the next level. Taking massive action is the answer. Action is the enemy of procrastination. Action is the enemy of paralyzing

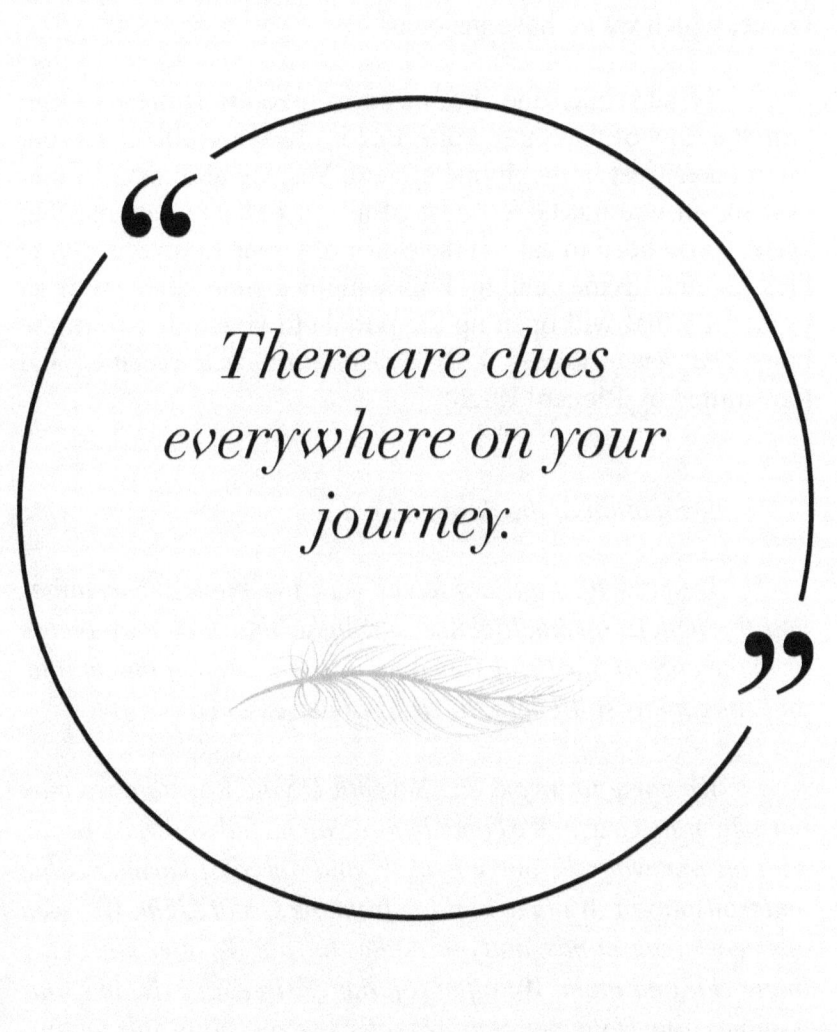

> There are clues everywhere on your journey.

fear and doubt. Clarity comes when you act. Clarity comes with engagement. Surrendering does not mean sitting around and doing nothing. To surrender means to stop controlling everything, relaxing and listing to the divine guidance, as you *move towards the direction of your dream with actions.* To surrender means to let go and trust the guidance and the inner voice of the Spirit of Grace, which we all have inside us.

To surrender does not mean to give up. It means to go with the flow of that inner voice that is always available to you, but it takes trust in the divine system. Yes, we all have an inner system, an internal GPS. Most of all, in order to activate that system, you need to call on the Spirit of Grace to invoke divine blessing and divine healing. Following is a short segment of an invocation that will open up the portals to Grace. It's from the book *The Seven Sacred Seals: Portals to Grace,* received and transmitted by Richard Rudd:

Invocation of the Seventh Seal

We seek to align ourselves with the highest harmonies and frequencies of intelligence and light, that they may pierce us to the core of our being, opening us to the arch of the infinite, and coaxing us softly into the arms of our essence.

We come to invoke the Seventh Divine Ray, that we may partake of its Grace. We come before you naked and vulnerable, with all our wounds, our mistakes, and our past karma visible and transparent. We hide nothing from the Great Light. We open our hearts, our minds, and our bodies to you. We offer you every living cell and atom. We offer you our desires, our dreams, our longings, our Holy intention. We offer you our Gifts, our talents, our Siddhis, our Divine Genius. We offer you our pain, our loss, our forgetting, our fear. We offer you our sadness, our anger, our lust, our selfishness, our denial, our shame, our cruelty, our guilt, and our indifference.

Especially we lay before you these many challenges of our humanity, for your transmutation. We lay our mortality before you.

We lay our life before you and come to you once again as a young child, a sweet innocent infant—before fear, before hope, before suffering.

We ask for your Divine Grace to begin dripping into our open, pure heart. We ask for your Grace to stroke our bodies, to rustle through the tiny hairs of our skin. We open our full being to your lustrous, wonderful, sweetening currents and emanations.

We invoke the shower of Luminescence—the Holy Light of this Seventh Ray.

We throw our heads up to the sky and open our arms wide to imbibe the mystery of this inner light. We let it run softly down our bodies, harmonizing our seven subtle bodies with its delicate web of woven light. We breathe in the royal cobalt blue of the luminescent beings, and their flashing gold scintillae, their blue/gold filaments, and their soft feminine light alights on us as though the great Mother herself had placed her sacred blue cloak upon our shoulders. We bow deeply to the presence of this Grace, this Holy Shakti that falls upon us from the celestial realms. We open our souls to the mystery of the dusk—to the moments of threshold in our lives. We embrace the wonder of the fading of the day into night, as the Holy inner light winds its precious way deeper and deeper into form and the first stars beckon and twinkle in the inner sky. We call it to ourselves, this luminescent light. We call its wonder and its Grace to go to work in our lives, to come and live with us, to create hidden passageways of harmony in the fractal tendrils of our life. We invite this Luminescent to sparkle our life with miracles, to open, to enliven, to inspire, to sanctify all those we know, see, hear, think about, and connect to.

. . . We breathe in your Grace. We open to its wonders, its mysteries . . . we allow ourselves to be a vessel of Grace. We affirm to work with the energy of our suffering. We understand through your Grace that our suffering calls us ever closer towards you. We understand through you that suffering is Grace. We imbibe this greatest of all human Truths—Suffering is Grace. We let this Truth resonate in every cell of our being. We let our DNA laugh aloud with its Truth. We are a passage towards the Divine, and our suffering is the river that leads us finally to the ocean of You, of I Am.

There's also a technique you can use to harness that power by activating the two hearts that we all have. It is through meditation on your Twin Hearts, the heart and the brain (divine heart). The energy center in your heart is the hotline to activate your brain's subconscious mind, which is connected to your crown chakra. This is where you can connect with your spiritual cord to connect with the divine and our soul.

So, if you're ready to test-drive this technique, read the steps below. Here's what I'd like you to do:

Twin Hearts Meditation Facilitated by Master Stephen Co of Pranic Healing

Master Stephen Co is an expert in Pranic Healing and Arhatic Yoga, an energy management system designed to empower people with personal development skills for greater health & well-being, a deeper spiritual connection, and living a practical and fulfilling life.

In this meditation I learned from him, we activate two hearts: our emotional heart, which is the heart chakra on our chest, and our spiritual heart on the crown chakra, which is the energy center for divine connection. What this does is flush out all negative energies. It's so simple, yet so effective and powerful.

> "The heart knows exactly what your soul desires. The heart has the strongest electromagnetic field. It manifests more powerfully."

This meditation, starts with a very simple invocation for divine blessings and divine protection:

To the Spirit of Grace, to all the Holy Angels, the Holy Teachers, spiritual masters, we humbly ask for your divine blessings, your divine love, divine mercy, and your divine protection. With gratitude, full faith, and total trust. So be it.

To facilitate the flow of energy throughout your body, curl your tongue off to the roof of your mouth. Close your eyes and relax. Breathe in and breathe out. Inhale brilliant light to every part of your body and exhale grayish dirty energy out of your body. Inhale joy and love and peace, and exhale anger, stress, and any negative emotion.

Now, visualize a brilliant ball of light on top of your head. Imagine your body as an empty bottle. Visualize the brilliant light above your head opening. Pour in liquid, brilliant light to your crown, flooding your brain with brilliant light. Picture the insides of your body with brilliant light: your heart, your lungs, your intestines, your liver, your spleen, your spine, your muscles, and your bones with brilliant light. Imagine the brilliant light pushing down any impurities . . . down, down, down, down, and out of your feet and into the earth. Inhale, and exhale down.

Now, visualize the ball of light on top of your head turning green. Imagine the green light pouring down into your whole body on the inside. Imagine the brilliant greenish light cleansing, purifying any negative energies from any cell, any organ in your body, and gently pushing it down out of your feet and into the earth. Inhale slowly and exhale any impurities down into the earth.

Now, visualize the ball of light on top of your head turning purple or violet. Imagine the violet light flowing through every pore, every cell, every tissue of your body, just flushing any remaining negative energies down, down, down, down, and out of your feet and into planet earth. Inhale, and exhale down.

Now be aware of the center of your chest. Imagine a beautiful flower, a beautiful rose in the center of your chest. Smile, with just a beautiful rose inside your chest. Visualize the face of a loved one inside the beautiful flower. Smile at this loved one. Tell them how much you love them, how much you care for them, and be still.

Now about two feet in front of you, visualize the planet earth the size of a baseball. From this beautiful rose in the center of your chest, I would like you to gently radiate beautiful pinkish light toward the earth and embracing it. I want you to share the love that's within your heart for this loved one to every person, every creature on the beautiful planet earth, and gently follow me with a very simple, a very universal prayer: *"Lord, make me an instrument of thy peace. Where there is hatred, let me sow love. Bless every person, every creature in the beautiful earth with love and peace, especially nations that are at war, your friends, your loved ones that are not getting along. Bless them with peace. Bless them with love. Where there is injury, let me so pardon."*

Think of all the people that have hurt you. Just bless them with the spirit of forgiveness. "Where there is doubt, let me sow faith. Where there is despair, let me sow hope." Think of the loved ones that you have that are going through hard times. Bless them with a new hope that things will improve. Visualize them rising out of their problems, feeling good about themselves, and succeeding in whatever they're doing. "Where there is darkness, let me sow light. Where there is sadness, let me sow joy." Visualize every person you meet every day smiling with happiness and with great joy.

Now, inhale gently. Lift a sensation from the center of the chest up, up, up to the top of your head on your crown area. Now, visualize a beautiful white lotus flower on top of your head. Just smile at it. See it open, revealing the face of somebody you respect very dearly. It could be a teacher, a saint, an angel, or an image of God to you. Either way, just put your love, gratitude, and respect with this person. Be still and just be aware.

Now, from this beautiful white lotus flower, gently project a brilliant white light toward the planet earth two feet in front of you, and just say from the heart of God, "May every person, every being, every creature in the beautiful planet earth be blessed with happiness, with joy, with peace, with goodwill, and especially the willingness to go out and do good. May every person, every creature, be blessed with good health, happiness, joy, and spirituality."

Now be still and just *be.*

Now, you will simultaneously bless the earth from the heart and the crown energy centers symbolized by the rose and the lotus flower. Gently radiate golden light from the heart area and from the crown toward the beautiful planet earth. And just silently say from the center of the heart of God through your heart into your crown, "May every person, every creature in the beautiful planet earth be divinely blessed with good health, with happiness, joy, and divine peace. May every person, every creature be blessed with loving-kindness, with peace, inner peace, with healing, inner healing, with goodwill, and the willingness to do good. So be it."

Just gently radiate golden light and see it illuminating every person, every creature on the beautiful planet earth, and allow yourself to be a powerful clear instrument of divine love, mercy, and compassion to this new world.

Continue to bless the earth from your heart and your crown. Let the love that's within you, the peace that's within you radiate to every person, every creature, anywhere and everywhere all over the planet earth.

Now, gently raise your awareness a few inches above your head, and visualize a beautiful golden flame radiating

> *Life will go on testing your graciousness.*

brilliant golden light everywhere. In your mind's eye, try to sense the quality of this flame, try to fill its vibration, its quality, and try to sense how this energy feels to you.

Try to put your complete awareness on this beautiful golden flame. In your mind's eye, just look at that flame and that flame alone. Put your complete awareness on that flame and let go. Only the golden flame. Only the golden flame. And let go. Let go. Let go. Let go.

Just be still and let go. Just a flame. And let go. Let go. Let go. Let go.

With your eyes still closed, slowly come back to your normal consciousness. Gently wiggle your fingers and your toes and just try to be aware of your body. You will now release excess energy you've generated. Just gently raise your hands facing forward with bent elbows and with the hands facing forward.

Again visualize the earth in front of you. Imagine brilliant light coming out of your hands, and just silently follow me. "May every person, every being on the earth, every creature on the earth, a beautiful mother earth be blessed with happiness, with great joy, with healing, inner healing, with prosperity in abundance, and spirituality." Bless your friends, your loved ones with good health, happiness, prosperity, and spirituality. Bless your job, your career with success, with advancement and progress.

Just radiate tremendous amount of beautiful light toward the planet earth and see it light up, and just say, "May the earth be blessed with light, with love, and with power. May every person, every being, every creature of the beautiful planet earth be divinely blessed with happiness, joy, and peace."

Now, let's silently say a thanksgiving prayer to the Supreme God, to all the Holy Angels, the Holy Teachers: "Thank you for the light, the love, and the power; especially thank you for the divine protection. We thank you."

As you finish this meditation, gently open your eyes with a beautiful and wonderful smile. To help facilitate the assimilation of this healing energy in your body, for the next five minutes please do some gentle stretching and some simple physical exercises.

6
The Power of the Heart

In French, heart is called "coeur," which means courage.

After attending my first personal development event, I feel like a veil has been removed. Also, my inner voice that guides me keeps getting stronger and stronger and giving me downloads. What's interesting to me is it often happens when water is running: when I'm in the shower or taking a bath or washing dishes or brushing my teeth. It is when I'm in the present moment not thinking about anything—not the past, not the future—but just being present and in a relaxed state.

This inner voice guided me to become a coach, although I hesitated for six months. I didn't want to become a coach. It was not my plan to become one. The invitation to become a coach kept getting stuck at the bottom of my recycling bin, which I empty every week. Somehow this invite was also a sign that I'd been ignoring. I kept picking it up and reading it every week before throwing it away in the bin. Finally, a month before coaching certification week, I suddenly realized I was being called. This was a calling! I hesitated for six months because I was busy with my new evolved business, and it did not make sense for me to spend on tuition when I just spent all my retirement savings on building **Skinworx.**

But I finally surrendered and trusted that this was the right path and that I was being called. I can feel the pull. After the five-day training to become a Certified High-Performance Coach, we did a meditation during graduation in which we put our hands on our heart, and that's when my fifteen-year old spirit showed up again like a hologram. This time she (my younger self) thanked me for hearing her and following through. My entire body began to shake when my spirit hugged me and congratulated me for listening to my soul and taking massive action. Buckets of tears flowed down my face, crying tears of *joy*. I've released stuck energies in my body through this process. It's so fascinating for me to look back at that event.

A few days after certification, I kept feeling this new sensation I'd not felt before. It felt like my heart was so wide open and felt like water was flowing out. I actually kept looking at my chest to see what it was. I didn't see anything, but the sensation was so unusual.

I can now feel the energy center of my heart when it gets activated, like something is oscillating, and I feel beyond happy. It is more than happiness. It took me awhile to realize that this sensation is *joy*. It's been a mighty long time since I had experienced *joy*. And now I can say it feels like an energy vortex spinning so fast—not beating fast, but spinning fast, like an electric fan oscillating from your heart. What a sensational feeling!

Physiology of the Heart

There are forty-one thousand specialized cells in your heart called sensory neurons (brain cells). These comprise a hotline to your subconscious mind. In the book *The Power of*

> *Life is short and you have only a certain amount of time to make your mark in this world. And that's all the more reason to get focused.*

the Heart, Robert Bulwer-Lytton says, "A good heart is better than all the heads in the world."

Have you ever made a rational decision and later said, "If only I'd listened to my heart"? When you ignore your heart's messages, you bury your dreams and extinguish your inner fire. When you are completely out of touch with your heart, you feel uncomfortable, you feel anxious, depressed, uneasy, because you are living on the surface, missing out on something. Whenever you feel frustrated, ask your heart to connect you to your deepest emotions—they are the spark of divine energy that is so vital to living with purpose.

Have you ever had a business idea that kept visiting your thoughts, and every time it popped into your head, you felt your heart warm up, but then you kept ignoring it, and then that business idea went away but revisited you in a year, every year, and you still didn't do anything about it? Then another person starts that business and you thought, "Hey, that was my idea."

When you don't take action, that gift will be given to someone else who might take action toward it.

What Happens When You Don't Listen to Your Heart?

It speaks to you in a language that you might or might not recognize. Renowned genius Albert Einstein said that the heart is the master and the brain is the faithful servant, but we live in a society that honors the servant and ignores the heart. The truth is that the heart is connected to your Higher Self, aka Higher Soul. The heart knows exactly what your soul desires. The heart has the strongest electromagnetic field. It manifests more powerfully. The heart does not live in drama. And it is the seat of love and compassion. Knowing this now, which one should lead your life?

I have ignored my own heart for decades. I remember several year ago when I experienced some signs and symptoms of irregular heartbeats. I went to see a cardiologist to examine what was going on. He performed an electrocardiogram and said my heart was normal and there was nothing to worry about. But I keep feeling this strange sensation like my chest was hit by a rock, and it happened at least once a day. The cardiologist reassured me that nothing was wrong, and that I needed to stop worrying.

I believe that the heart communicates to us in a way that might not be obvious, but we need to listen. And how can you tell what it's trying to communicate? In the next topic I will teach you a heart-brain harmonization exercise that's helped me a lot in receiving my soul's messages through the heart.

Ignoring the heart actually increases the risk of heart dis-ease. Metaphysically, a heart dis-ease means the heart is screaming out loud that you are on the wrong path or something within you needs healing. According to Heart Math Institute, the electromagnetic field of the heart energy center is five thousand times stronger than the brain.

After ignoring the messages from my heart, I developed anxiety and panic attacks. It slowly escalated to daily episodes, and it began affecting my work. At the time, I did not even know what was happening to me. All of a sudden, I would just experience this sensation of suffocation like there's no oxygen going into my brain and feel like fainting. My clients would notice that I looked nervous, and I would feel even worse.

That's when I decided I needed help. I searched for a psychotherapist but not my physician because I did not want medications. There was something I needed to deal with and heal within me, and that's when my healing journey began. I undertook six months of therapy, doing the inner work, doing the homework, and really taking massive action toward healing. I got sick and tired of being miserable for so long. At that point, I was emotionally spent, and that lit a fire under my tail, which made me go get help. It's funny how people will wait until they hit rock bottom before they finally do something. Rock bottom can be a beautiful place to begin a new life.

Exercises: The more intellect you use, the less intelligent you become. Intelligence is of the heart, intellect is of the mind. We need to learn to marry them. This is heart-brain harmonization. This exercise is a very simple yet powerful exercise to tap into your heart's intelligence; you can ask a question to your heart and really pay attention to what it has to say. But first I want you to get a pen and journal so you can write down five things you're grateful for and really add that emotion of gratitude. The emotion is the key.

Take three slow deep breaths. Inhale for six seconds, hold it at the top for three seconds, exhale for six. Do this three times. And breathe normally. Put your hands on your heart. Feel a genuine sense of gratitude and appreciation, think of someone that you love or a pet that you love so much.

Now ask your heart a question and wait for the answer. The answer to your question might sound like your own thoughts.

Conclusion: the heart-brain is the brain we must listen to, not the head-brain. The head-brain is simply the processor and can help us with logistics and calculations, and it protects us from predators. You need to learn to marry the two.

The amygdala in the brain is where fear, doubt, and worry originate. The heart knows everything.

> *All feeling is a journey.*

7
Entrepreneurship and Spirituality

"Who you might become is forever before you, beckoning you onward. What you might accomplish keeps whispering your name. However much of your potential you unleash, there is always more, just waiting to be tapped into. To become energized and refreshed with belief in your capacity to make a positive difference. To maximize the power of your potential to bring about good in the world. And—in so doing—to come alive."
—Carly Fiorina

I believe there is an entrepreneur in many of us. Entrepreneurship is in our DNA; for many of us, it is still waiting to be expressed and unleashed. And because it is about taking risks, many people are paralyzed by fear of taking that leap of faith. Entrepreneurship takes courage, grit, tenacity, faith, passion, and love. It takes perseverance, boldness, diligence, the desire to transcend the status quo, and, most of all, it takes Grace.

What is an Entrepreneur?

An entrepreneur is a person who organizes and operates a business venture based on a visionary dream, and assumes much of the associated risk, to make their dream come true. The word in French means "someone who undertakes a challenge." From another perspective, entrepreneurship is a life philosophy. It is about making an impact and embracing challenges.

The success of your business as an entrepreneur depends on the level of your spiritual strength, and not just your intellect or skill. Yes, business is an intellectual and strategic game, but what sustains you and your business is your spiritual strength. Therefore, you must be spiritually inclined and self-aware and mindful of your business in order to exceed the expectations of all the stakeholders and yourself.

Entrepreneurship is also leadership. The way you lead yourself and your team determines the level of progress of your business. Remember that "Assets make things possible, but people make things happen." If entrepreneurship is leadership, then it is also about problem-solving and unlocking the highest potential in others. Entrepreneurs inspire people to not just be good at their jobs, but to be good people. We need to care for their success at work *and* life, not just work. We must set high goals and demand greatness and growth from our team. Don't settle for sideways. Attempt to grow quarter after quarter, year after year. The bigger the growth, the more people you can help. The only limitless resource in the world is human potential. It's not time or money or skill or fame or beauty or charm. It's human potential.

What is the Difference Between Owning a Small Business and Entrepreneurship?

The key difference is that a small business is a limited-scale business owned and managed by an individual or a group of

> *Prosperity is like the water level inside your body. If you don't drink enough, you become thirsty*

individuals, whereas an entrepreneur is involved in the process of designing, launching, and operating a new business; developing its processes and procedures; developing ideas to sell the products/services; and building a brand, not just a product, in pursuit of growth, stability, and financial success.

While definitions of entrepreneurship typically focus on the launching and running of businesses, due to the high risks involved in launching a start-up, a significant proportion of start-up businesses have closed because of "lack of funding, bad business decisions, an economic crisis, lack of market demand, or a combination of all of these."

An entrepreneur acts on opportunities to translate inventions or technologies into products and services, recognizing the commercial potential of the invention and organizing the capital, talent, and other resources that turn an opportunity into a commercially viable business.

What is Spirituality?

Spirituality can mean different things to different people. For some, it's primarily about participation in organized religion. For others, it's a nonreligious *experience* that involves getting in touch with their inner spiritual selves through private prayer, yoga, meditation, quiet reflection, or time in contact with nature (*Psychology Today Magazine*).

"An instinct toward spirituality appears to be deeply ingrained in humans. People can't help but ask big questions—research shows that even declared skeptics can't stifle a sense that there is something greater than the physical world they see," they say.

What is a Spiritual Entrepreneur?

Unless we have a set of positive values at the core of our lives, our goals will be inadequate, selfish, and untrustworthy. Regardless what spiritual discipline you believe in, love is at the core and its final goal. The quality of being concerned with the human spirit or soul as opposed to material or physical things is the end game and what spirituality is all about.

Spiritual entrepreneurship is based in the concept of love and the common good. It is about the intentional determination of making an impact in other people's lives, and embracing and solving each challenge as they come.

A spiritual entrepreneur's approach is that he/she develop plans, ideas, and processes to grow his/her business, and helping employees, stakeholders, and communities, while blessing them with the fruit of his/her effort. Their mindset is on others first.

Spiritual entrepreneurs work to lead workers to freedom, reward, recognition, and hope. This gives people the knowledge and feeling that, through their meaningful work, they are making a difference in the world. A spiritual entrepreneur sees work, every day, as an opportunity to create, grow, discover, learn, challenge old ideas, and rearrange old ideas in a new way—a better way.

Being an entrepreneur is a way to fulfill your creative potential. Wise spiritual entrepreneurs understand at a core level that while they are adding value and quality to their lives, they intentionally also add value to the lives of everyone they touch.

A spiritual entrepreneur is a spiritually-minded leader who integrates the elements of an ethically motivated workplace into the organization's day-to-day operation and practices. The aim is to develop a socially responsible business environment, where the practicing of the common good is at the core of what he/she does.

I believe there's an entrepreneur in all of us. The difference is that true entrepreneurs are the ones willing to let it out, grab it like a wild mustang, jump on its back, and ride it. Entrepreneurs are risk takers, record breakers, difference makers. They get up early, stay late, and will everyone around them to be great. They're the ones who fuel our economy, fuel job growth, fuel innovation, fuel technology, and make the world a better place.

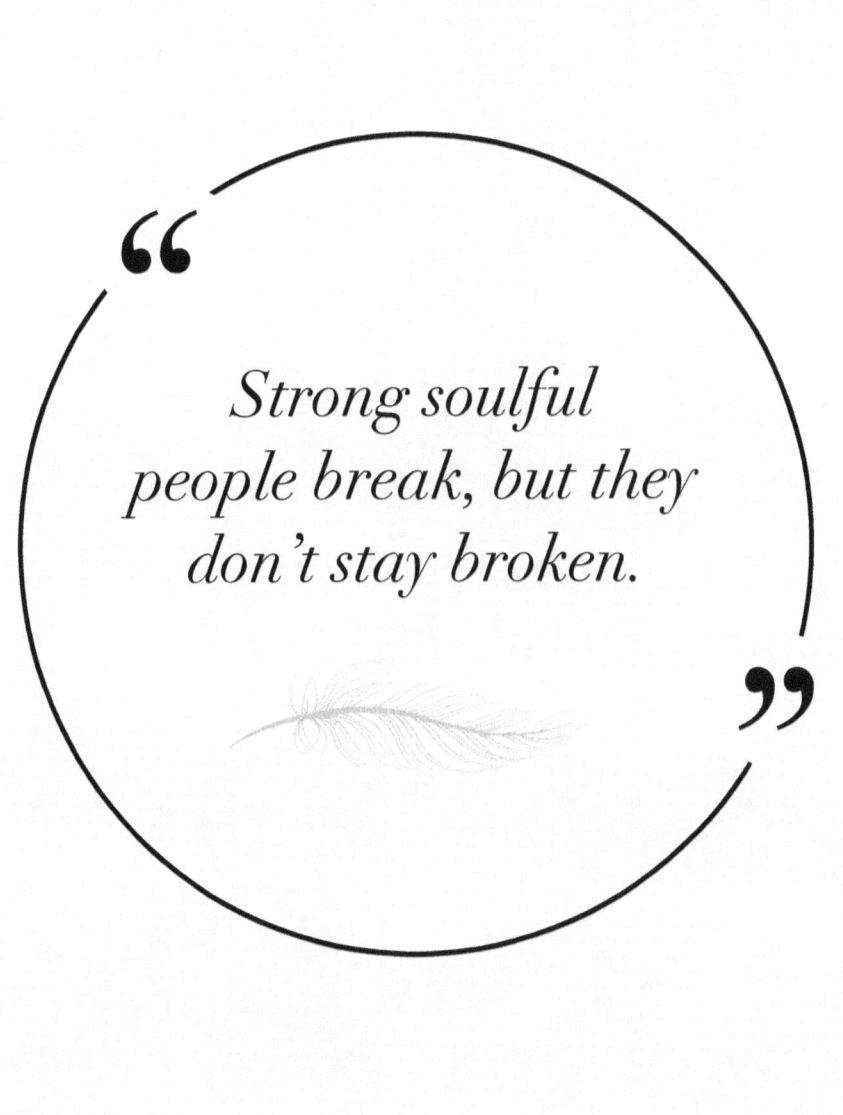

> *Strong soulful people break, but they don't stay broken.*

8
Money and Spirituality

One of the classic issues that traps our thinking is money. It can, literally, sabotage your entire life from ever being joyous or from ever feeling free. A classic cliché says, "Money makes the world go-round." It's kind of true. The way modern societies are set up, the current world economic model has its roots in the Middle Ages. Since free trade began its ascent, and as people pulled themselves out of the older hierarchical system and the first entrepreneurs were born, we've always had this bartering consciousness. But we never had such a complex system of accounting and taxes and all of that.

Here's another cliché: "The only certain thing is death and taxes." But we also existed before money. We existed without money in an earlier and simpler age, when we had no money at all. I'm sure we traded in goods or skills because that seems to be natural human behavior—to share, to exchange, to cooperate. But, in time, money became our currency and the means to do stuff and to relate with strangers or getting to know to trust or distrust, and to respect (or not respect) each other. And now we have a world that completely revolves around money. So, yes, it does make the world go-round, but it also makes our heads spin around. So how do we avoid that head spin?

Whether you're rich with more than enough money or struggling without enough money, you're still spinning. Money makes us spin. It drives us crazy. Do you know why? It's because money equates to time. "Time is money" (another cliché). So, whether you're rich or poor, money consumes your time, and in so doing it consumes your thinking. And it often makes your life more complicated (or so we think). But it doesn't have to be this way. Money is only a burden if you give it weight. It's the same with anything else. Money can either trap you or it can set you free. It's all a matter of what your inner attitude is toward it, and this is where money and spirituality meet. And these two things are not often comfortable bedmates.

I consider myself a spiritual person. I've always been fascinated by mysteries that we can't see, the invisible world that lies beyond our senses and physical world, or this empty space or other dimensions. The past few years I've been studying and exploring the hidden and the mystical. Along the way, I have studied with an esoteric group learning and practicing Pranic Healing. A lot of people have fallen into the wormhole of the spiritual world and have never been able to integrate their experiences to ordinary everyday life. If we cannot integrate the spiritual dimensions into the material world, I think at some level we've missed the point. I would even argue that we seem out of tune with where evolution seems to be heading. So, this is a great challenge.

The problem is we're split in so many things. The human brain tends to divide into religious and scientific, into male and female, into subjective and objective. But the contemplative approach unifies the polarities so you can only have a real balanced view of life when you look at it both scientifically and spiritually.

Our problem is time. Time is money. And that's very true for most people, but it's only true until you learn to slow down. Therefore, pause for a moment. For one moment in your day, take a break—pause! Stop in the middle of a task and take a few deep breaths. Just pause.

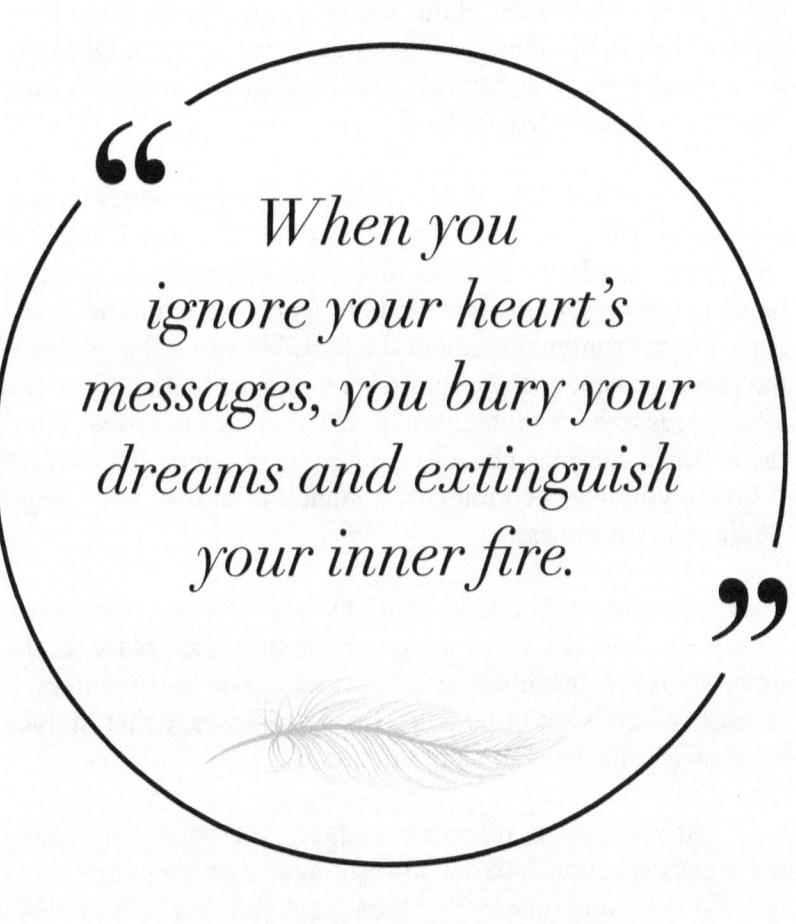

> "When you ignore your heart's messages, you bury your dreams and extinguish your inner fire."

Spiritual teacher George Gurdjieff calls this technique "self-remembering." Stake a claim and take back some time for yourself. Claim back some of yourself, every day. You don't have to be consumed by money. First, you have to see how deeply you've allowed yourself to become enslaved by money. Your ability to see how deeply you've become enslaved is in direct proportion to how much time you spend either thinking about money, worrying about money, or trying to make more money. This is the same whether you're rich or poor. Once you see through your fixation, then you can start claiming back large swathes of time for yourself.

We all have this illusion that having more money buys us more time. That's the most ridiculous thing I've ever heard. The only thing that buys us more time is awareness, which means being in the present moment and not worrying about the future. It means not ruminating about the past, but just being aware of the present moment and doing what you need to do now. Doing what needs to be done today will take care of tomorrow. That's the ultimate currency because it's free. It's current. It's the now. It brings you into the moment. So that's where we must begin. Begin with awareness.

People want to have more money because they want to have more time. But we're all looking in the wrong place for that time. We allow ourselves to be victims of our set of beliefs, or at least society's set of beliefs. But we can escape that rat race, because it's inside us. It's not out there.

It's a spiritual dilemma we face. And once you've done some introspection looking inward, and once you slow down intentionally and internally, then you can begin to breathe differently. That's when your concept of time will change. You will be able to "make more time." It's amazing that we can "make more time," but most people don't simply because they don't breathe properly. They don't breathe into their belly, and if you don't breathe deeply, you won't feel calm. And if you are not calm, then you can't make clear decisions, which means you won't really be operating at maximum efficiency. Money can be a means to breathing more deeply. Every time you think about money, picture it as an ally. Breathe down into your belly and smile. I bet you have never thought about money in such a way before.

Once you establish a healthy inner relationship with money, you can rebuild that relationship externally. You should be able to do that anyway because you construct and manifest your inner reality on the external plane, or, to put it another way, "As it is inside, it is outside." It just happens that way. This is why changing your beliefs and your views at the core—your inner level—changes everything in your outer level. You change the way you're imprinting your DNA and then you build a new life from the ground up. And what do you think that new life might look like? That's another thing worthy of contemplation. Write it down on a piece of paper. There's something powerful about writing things down.

A book by Richard Rudd, *The Gene Keys Golden Path (Book 3 of 4): Prosperity: A Guide to Your Pearl Sequence* talks about changing your inner relationship to money. It's about finding prosperity through *simplicity*. You see, prosperity requires simplicity; that's because prosperity is not the same as wealth. Wealth is top heavy. It creates an imbalance. Too much money makes you worry, again. It makes your life more complex, unless you give it away because, otherwise, you end up buying more stuff. You just do. And then, you have to manage all that stuff.

Prosperity is like the water level inside your body. If you don't drink enough, you become thirsty and your body doesn't operate properly. But if you drink too much, your body becomes bloated and other problems arise. The body has an ideal level of water it needs to run at maximum efficiency; money is like that. Each person must have the correct amount moving in and out of their life as a flow. When you find that flow, your worries are over. Most people never find that flow, and that flow is unique to each person. It's deeply connected to your breath. Therefore, we need to learn to pause, to breathe, to relax, and to then reconnect to that flow.

The opposing forces of nature can only be reconciled through asking the right question and then living the answer. So, what does all this have to do with money? You must realize that your own healing and your own fulfillment is tied into everyone else's. Everything in the universe is entangled at a "quantum level" with everything else. Thus, the deepest question you can answer in your life become: "How can I be of greater service to the whole?" If you make this question the foundation of your life and all your decisions, then your life will take you on a vast adventure. You will live your life, not someone else's life. You will live the highest life as well. You will unlock your higher life purpose.

Joseph Campbell is an American professor of literature at Sarah Lawrence College, in Bronxville, New York, who worked in comparative mythology and comparative religion. His work covers many aspects of the human experience. He has said, "Follow you bliss." He didn't say, "Follow your pleasure." He said, "Follow your bliss," because "Follow your pleasure" is the path that leads to misery. Bliss is in another dimension entirely separate from pleasure. To follow your bliss is to offer your life in service to something far greater than you. And that's the foundation of prosperity . . . Generosity.

> *Prosperity requires simplicity.*

9
Productivity

Your higher soul does not have hands and feet; you do. You need to do the work you were born to do. In order to fulfill your goals and dreams, you need to be effective, efficient, and productive. Many of you are busier now than you have ever been your whole career. Even though we all have big goals and dreams, most people today are drowning in stress, overwhelm, and uncertainty. There is so much urgency right now and so many people or projects vying for your attention. You might barely leave your office even for lunch. Maybe you have meetings all day with your team, staff, community leaders, and business partners. In between, you try to cram in email and/or social media. So much to do and so little time. You're up late every night doing more work. It's like working around the clock.

And yet you feel like you're not making enough progress, even though you're ticking off one task after another.

One of the worse feelings in the world is to be incredibly busy but feel that you're not making any progress. You're battling all the to-do lists and being everything to everybody, pleasing everyone, but your approach is wrecking your health or compromising your well-being. Projects seem to take forever. Progress comes too slow. Happiness seem so far away, a distant horizon never reached. Most of us have felt that at some point.

For many years I felt like a one-woman SWAT team. I finished each day with a lot of to-dos crossed off my list. What I learned was that not only was balance possible but so was increased progress. I discovered that sometimes all that busywork isn't my life's work. Sometimes, being effective isn't enough because achievement can be hollow if it gets out of sync with who you are, what you really want to be doing, what you're actually capable of. I had to learn the difference between just getting things done and reaching that higher soul-level productivity.

You need to have a very deliberate approach in planning your days, projects, and tasks. Like most productive people, spiritual entrepreneurs are good at setting priorities and working on what's important; they stay focused and avoid distractions and temptations. They are also more productive and yet also happier, less stressed, and more rewarded over the long term.

Spiritual entrepreneurs have found a way to produce more and also eat healthier, work out more, and still feel a greater love for taking on new challenges. And they don't just get more busywork done, they complete more activities and are more excellence driven. This is not because they are superhuman, over-caffeinated from Starbucks, or drink enough coffee to fuel a spaceship. So how is it that spiritual entrepreneurs produce more and also maintain their well-being and balance? It's because they have many deliberate habits. It's about habits.

In my own experience, I was once working full-time having to raise a daughter, attend grad school, and build a business at the same time. My dream was to have my own business and do what I love, and for me and my daughter to have a better life. I utilized every minute of the day wisely: Get up at 7

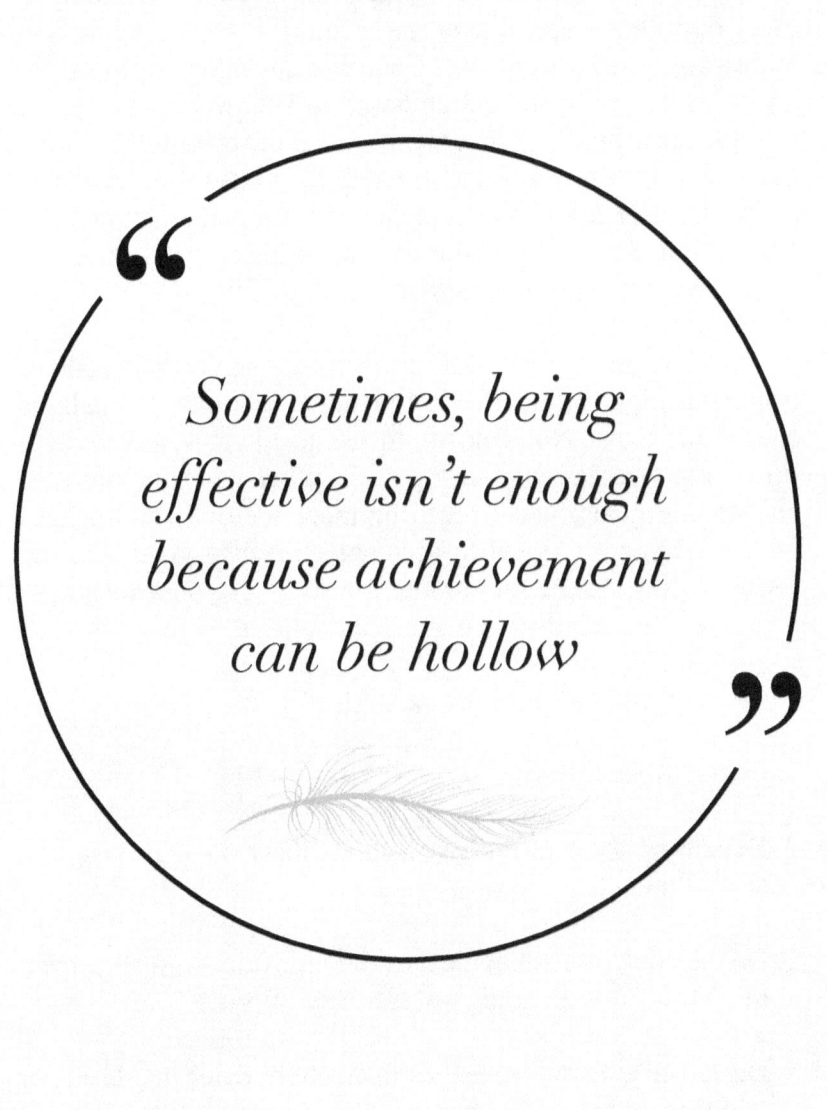

> "Sometimes, being effective isn't enough because achievement can be hollow"

am and prepare breakfast, shower, get dressed, get my daughter to school, get to work by 8:30 a.m. See patients until 4:30 p.m. Pick up my daughter at 5 p.m. Work out in my bedroom for a half hour. Prepare dinner by 6 p.m. Take a half-hour break. Help with homework. Grad school online from 8:30 p.m. till midnight, every day. Term paper due every Monday. Plan, create, design, build a business on Saturdays. Go to church on Sunday morning, go to brunch, go home and do homework since my term paper was due the next day. I eliminated a social life completely during those two years in grad school. Everything I did was scheduled and in the calendar. If it's not in the calendar, it doesn't get done. You need to SWAT team your days to be highly productive and achieve your goals and dreams.

Here are the productivity basics. The fundamentals of becoming more productive are setting goals and maintaining energy and focus. No goals, no focus, no energy—you're dead. Productivity begins with having goals. When you have clear and challenging goals, you tend to be more focused and engaged with what you are doing to accomplish. And it gives you this sense of flow. At the same time, it also gives you a feeling of enjoyment, especially when you accomplish a project.

It's really a simple process. Here it is:

1. Decide what you want.

2. Determine the five massive actions that will help you leap toward that goal.

3. Do the work on each of the five actions. At least do 60 percent of your workweek going toward these efforts.

4. Designate everything else as distraction, delegated tasks, or things to do in blocks of time in the remaining 40 percent.

So, test yourself. If I showed up in your office, could you show me your calendar and point out to me the blocks of time on your calendar that you structured to specifically complete your goal? If not, you know what to do next. "Block time" is a focus-management approach that requires "blocking out" significant amounts of time to advance or complete a major project in your life. It requires you to get clear on a major dream and schedule real time to leap toward it.

Life is short and you have only a certain amount of time to make your mark in this world. And that's all the more reason to get focused. What are you going to stop doing and what are you going to start doing that make your heart sing? Don't do things that make no impact. Determine what results really matter to you at this stage in your life, write down your five action steps to accomplish your big dreams, and go make it happen. You deserve your dreams and your dreams deserve you.

Productivity questions to ask yourself:

- When was the last time in your life you were the most productive? How did you get so much done then?
- Where do you feel you are not being productive in your life and why?
- What do you really feel is most important in your mission/career/achievements right now, and are you moving toward it at the pace you really want?
- What distractions or competing interests seem to keep you from getting more done, and how could you minimize them?

Fill in the blanks:

Dream Project #1 _____

Five big actions I must do to move this forward:

    1._____
    2._____
    3._____
    4._____
    5._____

Dream Project #2 _____

Five big actions I must do to move this forward:

    1._____
    2._____
    3._____
    4._____
    5._____

Dream Project #3_____

Five big actions I must do to move this forward:

    1._____
    2._____
    3._____
    4._____
    5._____

List the people you need to reach out to today no matter what:

_____
_____

List the people from whom you need something in order to move forward:

_____
_____

Priorities: The main things I must complete today, no matter what:

_____
_____

(Source: This tool is based on Certified High Performance Coaching, Burchard Group, LLC)

> *Signs bring hope and comfort when you feel alone and disconnected, or when you need encouragement.*

10
Spirit of Grace

We've all felt the soft touch of Grace in our lives. These are moments that lift us up when we've fallen. They are moments of Grace. The gift of graciousness means that whatever you do in life, you always consider the feelings of others. This is one of the great social gifts. Grace has a huge capacity to completely transform your life and the lives of everyone you meet. It's also about touching their hearts and even their souls. Graciousness means that you act with grace and consideration in everything you do.

The Spirit of Grace is extremely powerful in its effect upon others. The Spirit of Grace can greatly help others free themselves from their negatively charged emotions. There is a profound kindness at the core of this gift that can elevate others beyond their normal consciousness to states of love, laughter, or tears. For this reason, many people connected with this gift assume artistic, musical, creative, or entrepreneurial and vocal roles in life, where they can influence others through their natural social grace.

On the opposite end, people at the lower aspects or at the shadow level of Grace do not acknowledge their accountability for what they say or do. The opposite of Grace is dishonor. Dishonor is the shadow of Grace.

What does it mean to dishonor someone? What does it mean to dishonor yourself? Those two questions are ever connected. Dishonor runs deep. We dishonor ourselves every time we don't accept the way we feel. All feeling is a journey. And your suffering is a journey, and you have to begin with the knowing that you must honor it. You must even honor dishonor at some level. This lower aspect, the shadow level you always revert to, is a victim status. If you don't stop and look, how will you ever see your patterns? Don't try and run from your programming. You have to face it. You have to deal with it. You have to be accountable for your feelings, your thoughts, your self-judgments. And then you have a chance of letting go of your self-judgments. You have to have the chance. It's a process of awareness; that's all. It's simple. Contemplation really really helps you see these things because it gives you the space. It gives you the pause necessary to see the issue at hand.

We have to accept our shadows. It really is a huge challenge for humans. Life is about learning to be accountable for one's own state. But more often we usually blame another person. We don't take responsibility for our own state. We look for a reason. You see, it's not so easy to account for yourself because your own issues get tangled up with the issues of others. This is the dilemma. We aren't comfortable being uncomfortable. So we deflect our awareness in some way out of the present moment.

Dishonor is about us first. You dishonor yourself whenever you blame anything for anything because there's no fault. We aren't perfect; we make mistakes. We just have to be honest about it. This honoring the pattern itself begins the process of transformation. It cries out over and over for your attention, for your awareness, and you just have to learn how to let it in. It's just self-honesty. That's all that's needed. This is all about the emotions. This is a great emotional vow.

> *Believe that you are guided and supported and that you deserve your dreams.*

Graciousness is so beautiful. It's so practical and so simple. It's the path to Grace, after all. It will save your life. It will save anyone in any situation anywhere. It's a whole cocktail of noble qualities. It's also very refined and often very subtle because it's an attitude carried in your aura rooted in a deep reverence for all life. It all stems from your ability to be accountable because when you're accountable for your own aura, for your own chemistry, for your emotions, then you move in such a clean way through the world because all your accounts are settled as you go along. You don't allow debt or negativity to build up.

The Gift of Graciousness might also be called the Gift of Soul. Soul is when you begin to emanate the quality of your essence. It's the refining of your emotions. When your soul really shines out, you will even begin to let go of the need for pleasure, and then you become grateful for whatever life brings. That's another quality inherent in graciousness: gratitude. When you feel grateful to life, it's because you're so aware of death, and so your priorities are transformed. And so if you let go of pleasure, so you let go of pain. You become more accepting of life and its rhythms. This is what graciousness brings you. You're no longer a victim of the pleasure-pain song. To live with equanimity is to live life lightly but, at the same time, deeply. That means you pay attention but you have an unquenchable inner calm. Graciousness is the process of bringing Grace into form. Graciousness invites Grace. It doesn't exist without challenges. It thrives on challenges.

Life will go on testing your graciousness. It needs to be tested so that you can refine it. How graciously do you treat yourself? How graciously do you treat others? It's honest. It has a soft touch. It carries a story with depth and humor, but it isn't perfect. It's just human. True graciousness can be really gritty. It can be rough around the edges. Graciousness carries a kind of cosmic kindness inside of it. When you're gracious, you often hold back from saying something you might have otherwise said because it might stir someone up. You don't allow your own issues to get tangled up with theirs. So when you stop judging yourself, then you're no longer going to judge others. And we learn to be careful without being fearful. And we learn to be warm without being overbearing. And we learn to be candid without being cruel. It's a balancing act. It's a transformational field in which we are steadily refined. It's all because we learn to stop dishonoring ourselves at the very deepest level. You see, it's all about really owning your own stuff. It's about treating yourself and others with dignity no matter how they behave.

Sometimes Grace just falls on you and you can't predict when it can occur. And you can't do anything to make it happen, but you can prepare the ground through the way you deal with difficulties and with graciousness. We have a term for this, "a fall from Grace," and it's poignant because Grace is often about how we deal with the shadows, how we deal with our mistakes. It all comes back to accountability. We have to deal with our falls as cleanly and openly as possible. Grace is buried in every shadow. It's a gift given to us to open us up to another possibility.

The more grateful we are, the more Grace appears. They are to be savored. It must be allowed to mature inside us.

The Gift of Graciousness might also be called "the Gift of Soul." This is the ability to live life to the full, holding no feelings back, while at the same time having deep respect for the feelings of others. If you're fortunate enough to tap into the higher qualities of the Gift, your life can be filled with art, music, romance, deep relationships, and enchantment. But above all else this is the Gift of living life from a place of deep love and soul.

This contemplation on Grace is by Richard Rudd, author of the book *Gene Keys: Unlocking the Higher Purpose Hidden in your DNA (2009)*.

11
Your Soul Must Endure Challenges

Courage is resistance to fear, mastery of fear, not absence of fear."
—Mark Twain

Courage is not formed in absence of fear. And strength is never formed in absence of challenges. Strong soulful people fall, but they don't stay down, they get right back up. Strong soulful people break, but they don't stay broken. They heal and they piece themselves back together and they come back stronger. They are relentless. They sometimes might feel like quitting, but they don't. Strong soulful people aren't free from challenges. They are strong because of the challenges.

Helen Keller once said, "Character cannot be developed in ease and quiet. Only through the experience and trial and suffering can the soul be strengthened, vision cleared, ambition inspired, and success achieved." Whatever you've been through, trust that it was sent for a purpose. Look back and think about how it made you stronger, wiser, or better. Use the pain of your past to create a better future for yourself. Build a business that generates an impact for the higher good. There's a saying: "I've never met a strong person with an easy past." They are strong because their past was not easy. But through the pain in that struggle came strength. Through the hell came qualities from heaven. They went through the darkness and found the light. When you're down, understand that this moment will pass. Oh, yes, it will!

When things seem impossible, know anything is possible if you keep going. Then if you feel like you have no strength inside, dig a little deeper in your soul and discover what it is that's really inside. *Trust that whatever is happening in your life is for a reason and a purpose.* Trust there is a gift in every situation, find that gift, and then release it. Know that through this struggle, you will get stronger and your soul must endure. You will be wiser. You will be better. To be human means to have shadows or challenges. To be human means to experience highs and lows, light and dark, and it is in those low and dark moments that character is formed. It is in those low and dark moments . . . in refusing to quit . . . in marching on . . . that strength is formed. You must go through that darkness to find the light you are truly looking for, because it's on the other side of that. You must face this dark side because there's a lot of energy in there. There is actually goodness in there that you can use to find greatness.

"You can't find that peace you're looking for, until you have overcome yourself."
—David Goggins

If you can find the strength, think about all that is good in your life, everything you are grateful for, know that the good is stronger than your challenges, and keep fighting because of that good. Keep fighting for those you love. Keep fighting for you. You have so much more to give and so much more to live. This is such an example to set—when you're down, understand that this moment will pass. When things seem impossible, know anything is possible when you keep going.

So many of us suffer from uncomfortable symptoms in our lives—depression, anxiety, addictions—which affect our life

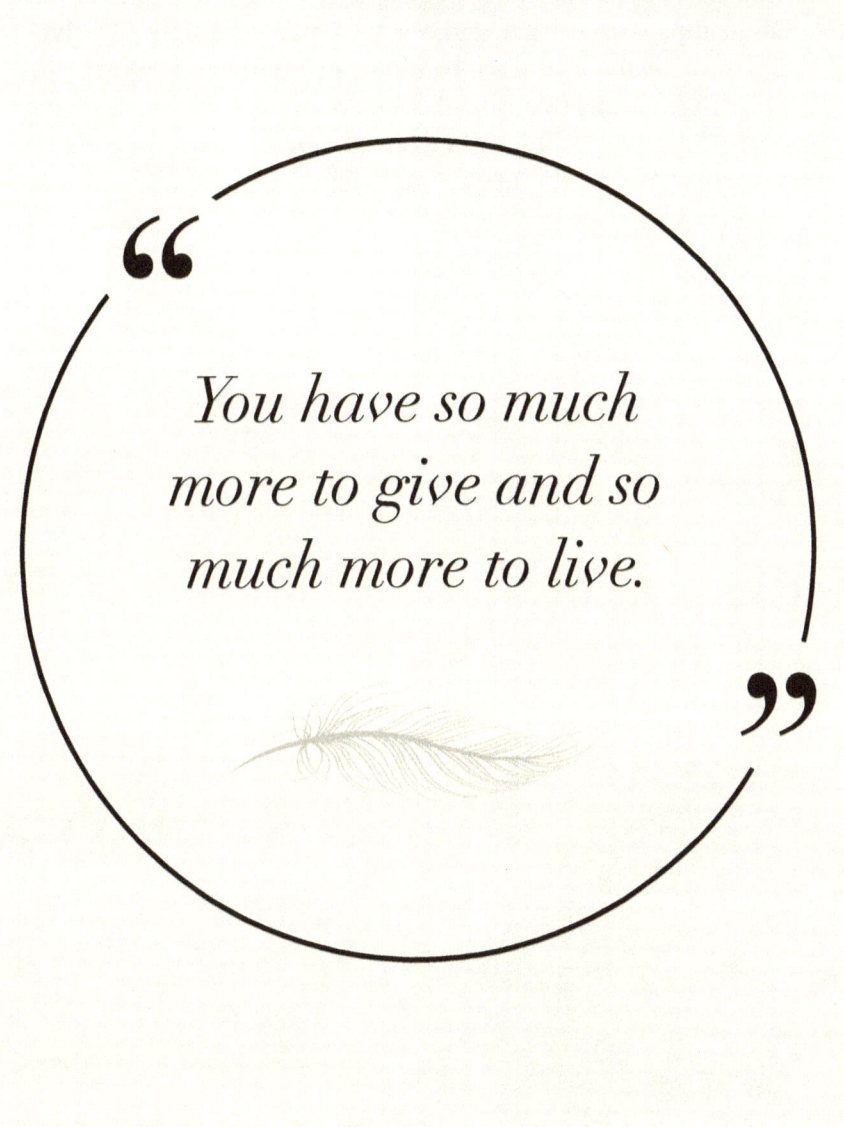

"You have so much more to give and so much more to live."

and business. It is believed that these symptoms arise from loss of connection to the soul. Basically, there is conflict between our inner selves and outer lives. Fortunately, the soul has a natural instinct to heal. It is constantly communicating with us and telling us what it needs through our bodies, our feelings, our relationships, our dreams, and our art. Once we attune ourselves to our soul's language, deep healing can begin to take place. So, keep going, because your soul needs to endure this challenging journey. And don't forget to have fun along the way. Celebrate the small wins and not just the big wins.

12
How to Take What You Learned into the World

My vision for those who are ready to get to their next level is to finally step up and take massive action toward their own healing, vitality, and transformation in order to build something they've always dreamed of and really live a vibrant, joyful, and fulfilling life.

- Reconnect with the wisdom of your heart and body, and trust your own instincts.
- Re-ignite your passion and create the business you've always dreamed of.
- Reclaim your personal power.
- Release the hurts you hold in your heart, and open up to forgiveness, compassion, and love.
- Rediscover your creative expression and find your authentic voice.
- Reawaken your intuition and imagination, and gain heightened insight into your life.
- Remember your spiritual connection and find a sense of sacredness in your life.
- Release blocked emotional energy that's been holding you back in your life.
- Re-tune and re-balance your energy centers, restoring your whole energy system to a healthier state of vibrancy and balance. Let go of what no longer serves you and awaken strengths that have been lying dormant within you. Slowly but surely, you'll start to discover your personal power, heal what you need to heal, live energized, and create the life you've always wanted.

May the Spirit of Grace be with you always.

Soulworx, An Open Invitation

If you feel intrigued, inspired, and enthused, consider signing up and joining us in our upcoming live event experience, **Soulworx Academy.**

Visit www.MySoulworx.com to learn more.

Contact Cheryl Pierce, RN, MSN
Cheryl@MySoulworx.com
to book her for
speaking engagements,
workshops, retreats, trainings

---

 mysoulworx • myskinworx
 mysoulworx

Skinworx, San Francisco—
Come and visit us where we
Inspire Confidence
through Better Skin.

Visit www.MySkinworx.com to learn more.

About the Author

Cheryl Pierce believes confidence is a vital part of this magical element called happiness. Her mission is to inspire confident and joy through better skin. Specialized in wound care, she was fascinated with how the body is designed to heal despite large gaping wounds. Her Skin to Soul program is a culmination of her 23 years of healing work as a Registered Nurse and a Certified Public Health Nurse.

Graduating in 1996 from University of San Francisco with a Bachelor of Science in Nursing. She received her Certified Wound, Ostomy, Continence Nurse 2005, Metropolitan State University in St Paul, MN. And worked as a Wound Care Consultant at Sutter Health organization. In 2010, she obtained her Master of Science in Nursing from the University of Phoenix. Certified Trained in the advanced techniques of Botox and dermal filler administration through the Aesthetic Enhancement Institute.

In San Francisco, 2007, she founded, and became CEO of Ageless Beauty Skin Clinic, Inc. In 2016, it evolved into Skinworx, with a mission of inspiring confidence through better skin. As an avid lifelong learner, Cheryl continued her personal and professional growth and development, learning to master her psychology, physiology, productivity, presence and purpose. She became a Certified High Performance Coach in 2016. Guest Speaker at San Francisco State University Business School. MBA class of 2017. Studied at Tony Robbins Business Mastery I-II, Leadership Academy, Life & Wealth Mastery, UPW, Date with Destiny, 2018-2019. Studied at Master Stephen Co: Advanced Pranic Healing. Kriyashakti and Spiritual Business Management, 2019. Speaker at New Living Expo, San Mateo. Topic: Entrepreneurship and Spirituality. 2019.

www.ingramcontent.com/pod-product-compliance
Lightning Source LLC
Chambersburg PA
CBHW030331100526
44592CB00010B/650